CONTE

FOREWORD

I've known James as a writer of interesting and insightful work stories for many years and as an internal communicator who never fails to bring new ideas to address the most obvious yet challenging problems we find in our workplaces.

He wrote a thought piece about the art of followership. He felt it needed writing and he was right. It was extremely well received and prompted much debate within our organization. So, I dared him to write a book about more of his ideas and unique perspectives. A year later, *Workability* is born.

What I like about *Workability* is that it offers workable answers to everyday people challenges. James's hard-earned experiences across a range of organizations in different sectors are sources of real-world examples. *Workability* will resonate with anyone, no matter what their level, because what James shares are all things we wished we had known when starting out in our working lives, but which many of us still struggle with years later.

Workability is a collection of reflections dealing with the very essence of what it is to be human in the workplace. James's practical yet humorous voice cuts through to the things that matter because he is brave enough to take a stance, sometimes controversially. You may disagree with some of what you'll read, but it will challenge you to ask yourself why.

I have spent much of my life mentoring others of all levels to help find their own way. This book offers any aspiring professional an ample amount of wisdom in such a personal journey.

Speaking as a former president of the International Publishers' Association, a great many books have come across my desk and I assure you that, of its type, this sits among the best of them.

YOUNGSUK (YS) CHI
Director of Corporate Affairs, RELX and Chair, Elsevier

INTRODUCTION

I started my working life a mile underground in southern Africa chasing veins of gold. It was the logical choice for a degree-qualified mining geologist. But quite different from the south London streets in which I grew up. Apart from the colourful language perhaps.

Since then, I've worked in retail, waste, food, renewable energy, construction, oil & gas, not-for-profit, security, prisons, consulting, telecoms, investment banking and today, information & analytics.

Some of these organizations have been global. Some with hundreds of thousands of employees. One was housed in a single room hidden away behind the Palace of Westminster in London. One was based in Portakabins. I've seen all sorts.

Quite by accident, a few years into my working life, I found that I was good at explaining complex issues in a way that the media, local communities and colleagues could understand. Before I really knew what was happening, I found myself working in corporate communications.

With time, I became increasingly fascinated with the human condition and how it plays out at work. I delved deeply into psychology, human behaviour and language. I then started to apply these learnings at work and developed employee communication and engagement approaches before the discipline even had a name. Today, internal communication is recognised as a primary enabler of organizational performance.

I've led people, led teams and led more projects than I can recall, helping many large organizations through market-defining mergers, major crises and massive upheaval. In my time I have worked with some truly exceptional people and have been part of award-winning corporate communications teams.

Some of us choose corporate life. Others, like me, just kind of end up here. In either case, it's not always plain sailing. I have found that it's not what you do at work that's hard. It's how you do it. Which means working with people who just see the world differently than you do. It sounds easy when I write it. But it isn't.

In this book I have brought together a collection of stories to bring new perspectives to common challenges we all face at work. Aiming to share ideas that you can use today. Despite my rich and varied experiences, I have never considered myself the finished article in terms of my skills at work. And I still don't.

1. PEOPLE

MANAGING OTHERS IS A MESSY BUSINESS

I thought long and hard about the subtitle of this chapter and decided that after all is said and done, managing other people often is a messy business. In the most glorious and positive ways people are driven by emotion, which makes them unpredictable. And with all the systems and processes in the world to control how things are supposed to happen at work, they rarely go the way we think they will because we fail to factor in the human impulse.

It's this capriciousness which makes the whole process of managing people exciting and fascinating for those with curiosity about the human condition. But a complete nightmare for those without. And don't forget, it's not just your people who are unpredictable, emotional, impulsive and capricious. You are too.

The unfortunate reality is that most aren't put in charge of managing people because they are good at it. It's because they are good at precisely something else, so they are woefully ill-equipped and then must learn on the job. I once witnessed a superstar salesperson take over a large team only to fail miserably within six months. He struggled to adjust from being a lone-wolf hunter of new business to someone who needed instincts more akin to farming to build a cohesive team more effective than the sum of its parts. We've all seen this happen one way or another.

Based on my nearly 60,000 hours of working life and experiences of directly managing around a hundred people in a whole host of different environments, I have condensed into a few thousand words the priorities that matter most when managing others. My aim is to bring you grounded, practical insight that you can either use right away, or at least give you something meaty upon which to ponder.

Your number one priority

The best managers of people I have seen have one single thing in common. They are all highly self-aware. They know and are comfortable with themselves, so are fundamentally better placed to know others, which, in turn, means they know how to get the best out of them. They understand their own emotions so are better able to work with the emotions of others. Displays of emotions in the workplace for these people are okay.

By contrast, the worst managers of people I have seen are people who think their technical knowledge and perceived hierarchical power are all they need to make others do what they want them to do. And we all know how well it works out for people like that.

So, if you are struggling to get the best out of your team, the chances are that you will first need to attend to the development of your own self-awareness. Now, some people are naturally self-aware, like some people are natural jugglers. But few are, many don't bother to learn and those who do, often give up before they have mastered it.

One of the defining moments early in my career was when the company I worked for reorganized and I had a new boss. I had never come across anyone like him before. He treated me as an equal from the get-go and spent time really getting to know me and the others in his new team. It was a big group scattered all over the country. It took quite some time.

I asked him why he invested so much effort in us. 'It's not what you do at work that's hard, it's how you do it', came the response. And this was from someone who cut their teeth in the space industry, which sounded pretty hard to me.

And hasn't his insight been right every single day of my working life? It's how you do things, not what you do, that's hard. And the how specifically refers to how you relate to others and work with them.

'The best managers of people are all highly self-aware. They are comfortable with themselves, so are fundamentally better placed to know others, which, in turn, means they know how to get the best out of them.'

Depending on what you do for a career, you may think your number one priority is to grow revenue, develop innovative products for customers, better equip the organization with technology, hire the best people or ensure your organization complies with the law. If you do any of these things or thousands of other things besides, but you also manage people, then your number one priority is to ensure their welfare before anything else.

Managing people is a bigger responsibility than you probably think it is. Without, of course, denying the individual responsibilities everyone has while at work, as a line manager you are entrusted with your people's safety, health and wellbeing at work. It's your job to make sure that they can be themselves without fear of judgement, that they can have a life outside and never have to apologize for it, that they can feel supported, trusted and valued, and, most importantly, that they can become successful in ways that are meaningful for them. If you don't do these things, then you are firstly failing in a basic societal precept and then you will find that you fail in everything else you are trying to achieve.

This means investing time in getting to know your people at a human level. Where have they come from? Where do they want to go, if anywhere? How do they want to get there? What do they care about? Who and what matters in their life? Why do they work here? What makes them tick? And then being prepared to share these things about yourself. Such rapport builds your ability to influence.

I've never met anyone in my entire working career who came to work to make a mess of it. It's just that as line managers we sometimes fail to take account of beautiful individuality and the tensions it can cause, then work with those tensions to generate new ideas and new ways of working.

People join organizations but leave their line manager. So, managing people well is the first line of defence in employee retention and it's the single most important responsibility you have at work. It is my own experience and my observations of what successful managers do that if you look after your people, the rest will come. It is one of my universal truths in the workplace.

Make your people famous

But taking a distinctly human approach to managing your team is not enough. Your work is not yet done. There's more to do and that means letting go of your own insecurities and creating the right environment for your people to overtake you. If you don't feel that upward pressure, then what on earth will keep you on your toes and drive you to perform better?

This starts with hiring people who have the potential to be better than you. Then unlocking that potential so they are at your heels pushing you onwards. It takes no small amount of humility and a healthy slice of courage to think this way.

You might think you can control your team. But it's an illusion. If you rely on control, then you are playing on people's fears. Fear of failure, fear of losing their job, fear of losing their status. And fear is the fire blanket for success. It snuffs it out.

If your people flounder, then so do you. Every time. It's the ultimate weakness of any team leader to fail to help their people develop to become more successful than they are.

By contrast, of course, if you create the right environment for your people to shine then not only can you feel good about what you have helped make happen, but that brilliance will reflect on you. Even as I write this, I cannot quite believe so many people still do not understand this simple truth.

Your job is to help open doors for your people. Let them become successful in their own right and let them make a name for themselves inside your organization and beyond. To help them work out their own solutions so they take ownership rather than simply doing what they are told to do.

Few of us in the corporate world really have any chance to leave a lasting legacy. But something we can all do, when managing others, is to help them fulfil their potential, so they in turn model your behaviour and help others in their own way. That, to me, sounds like a worthy legacy for anyone at work and one that a great many of us can achieve. If you can't get your head around this, then maybe you shouldn't be managing people at all.

The three ways things go awry

This is all well and good. But how do we react when things go wrong? Which they invariably will. This is the real test and one that, as a manager of people, you must pass with flying colours. In my experience there are three main areas where things go wrong in the dynamic between team leader and team member. The first, and by far the most common, is when we simply see things differently. The second is when something isn't working the way you expected, and the third is when, despite best endeavour, sometimes people's behaviour lets them down. Let's take these in turn.

Simply seeing things differently

One thing we can all be sure of in this life is the way we see things is not shared by anyone else. So, despite your best efforts to gain agreement or clarity there will always be different views. And this is simply because our map of the world is different from everyone else's.

But the map is not, as they say, the terrain. Which means as a manager of people you need to walk in their shoes, see what they see, feel what they feel and hear what they hear. Explorers don't learn how to explore by looking at maps. They put on their boots. As Bilbo Baggins says in *Lord of the Rings*: 'It's a dangerous business, Frodo, going out your door. You step onto the road, and if you don't keep your feet, there's no knowing where you might be swept off to.'

And so it is when managing people. You have to get out there. You must invest time to better understand their world, so you have some chance of being able to influence it and for them to see that you care enough to try. This now brings us to the second case.

When something isn't working the way you expected

I am a firm believer that to acknowledge a behaviour is to reinforce it. Focusing on the positives and largely ignoring the negatives has huge power if you are prepared to be a little patient. You may need to adjust your resources to manage areas where your team member may not perform as you would perhaps like or you may need to provide learning opportunities to help them. But in practice, just acknowledging and rewarding the behaviour you want and ignoring the one you don't can create sustainable and long-term changes.

I tend almost entirely to focus on the positives of my team members' performance and let the negatives, as I see them, work themselves out. In any case, who am I to actively pick people's behaviours apart and try to reconstruct them in some utopian generalization of what constitutes good?

When bad behaviour gets the better of someone

And, finally, to the third case. People don't mean to mess up, it's just sometimes they do. How does the team leader who has come this far deal with the real messiness that can result from bad team member behaviour? The kind of behaviour that puts the organization's reputation at risk and needs to be urgently addressed.

The simple answer is it must be dealt with in real time, there and then, but not in front of others. It must be specific in terms of their behaviour so they can clearly understand what they did and what impact it had on other people or on the organization. This is most important, as without it the recipient may well have no idea what it was they did or why it even caused an issue. Because, don't forget, their map is simply different; they aren't trying to make a mess of things.

Your feedback to the recipient must also be delivered calmly and decisively with a crystal-clear end message of what specific behaviour needs to change, why and what the consequences will be if it doesn't.

These are not the kind of conversations that can wait for an end-of-year performance review. In fact, once dealt with effectively as described above, they should not be mentioned in any annual assessment. Raking up missteps is not the way to move forward.

These are difficult conversations for sure, but as the Peter Parker Principle from *Spiderman* tells us: 'with great power, comes great responsibility'.

Who doesn't want to be recognized?

I have been involved with a great many employee opinion surveys in my time across a range of organizations in different sectors. In almost all, a significant proportion of employees tell their employer that they could do better in rewarding them for the effort they put in: fair reward for work done.

Maybe this is another one of these universal truths at work. No matter how much someone is paid, they always feel like it should be more? There is some logic to this thinking. After all, if you ask people the question, then what else would you expect them to say, really?

Good people will always take on more responsibility as they build their career, so they may well feel a little behind in what they are paid as they add more to the organization. Which is why benchmarking reward is so important.

Many of us will have taken on new team members who have already been with the organization for many years. If we look, we may well find that their reward has drifted out of kilter with their evolved role and with the market. I don't want us to get caught in a long discussion here about reward processes, but the one thing I would say is to ensure that your people's roles are regularly benchmarked with the market. Otherwise they will fall behind, which means your organization will be inadvertently exploiting them and so will you. They will find out, sooner or later, that they are off market value which will either disengage them or make them leave. Both of which are passive outcomes for the people manager aspiring to do better.

But what I really want to focus on in this section is the power of recognition. You have read why we need to make our people famous earlier in this chapter but here I want to expand on this idea with some simple approaches.

You need to be there for your people and available for them. Making time to listen to them. How else will you be able to see their achievements and recognize them for their efforts?

And you need to take positive steps to recognize them. Firstly, by saying thank you and often. Even when they are just doing what they are supposed to be doing. It reinforces the value in tasks that can seem repetitive or mundane, especially when you reinforce why what they do matters. It never ceases to amaze me how many people say they never receive any thanks for doing their work.

Secondly, by praising good work in front of others, they gain peer recognition. Who doesn't like that?

And thirdly, if no other formal mechanisms exist, seeing what you can do within the rules to recognize and thank them by giving them some time back. It is my experience that people value time above all else.

If you manage people in real time like this, it means that reviewing performance becomes more organic and just part of doing work each day. If your organization has a formal review of annual performance, then even this should become a more useful and positive process for all parties involved. There are no surprises or unhelpful regurgitation of any mistakes from which people have moved on. It becomes a more positive discussion where successes can be reflected upon, recorded and celebrated.

A pile of calculators

We come to the end of this chapter with a story. Back in the mists of time I worked for a relatively small company. The performance of the business was under pressure and before looking to make any roles redundant the managing director personally drove a cost reduction programme. She saw wastage across the business and asked around a hundred or so colleagues in the head office each to do their part. Small gestures, she said, would add up and we should do our bit.

Despite huge efforts out in the operations of the business to save money, the head office lagged behind. So, one Monday morning we all came into the office to find a pile of over a thousand office calculators on the floor in reception. The managing director had asked the office manager to collect them from all the desks and drawers.

She left a handwritten message on top of the pile. It said something like: 'I asked you to do your part. You didn't. There are over a thousand calculators here for a hundred people. This wastage is not helping. You need to do better. If you don't, I will do it for you.' She was right. And we all knew it. She could do all our jobs.

Here was a leader who lived and breathed her company. She was known by everyone and had worked her way through the business. She never asked anyone to do anything that she wasn't prepared or capable of doing herself.

And here's the lesson I have taken forward in my career of managing people: you should never ask team members to do things you are not only prepared to do yourself, but also capable of doing yourself. It's all too easy to take the elevated and expansive position of someone who shapes the agenda and have no idea how your team actually does what it does. But that detachment hinders understanding and does nothing to show your interest in their work.

If you have someone in your team who does something you have no idea how to do, ask them to show you. And just watch how their respect and loyalty grows.

2. FOLLOWERSHIP

KNOWING HOW TO FOLLOW IS MORE
IMPORTANT THAN KNOWING HOW TO LEAD

It's estimated that there are over 15,000 books in print on corporate leadership in the English language alone. And many more out of print sitting on shelves in forgotten corners of offices all over the world with pages slowly foxing.

I started work in the 1990s. Germany was reunified, Nelson Mandela was released from prison, the Hubble space telescope was launched and *Encyclopaedia Britannica* saw its highest ever sales. And the decade when Tim Berners-Lee created the world wide web, even though I was just getting to grips with a fax machine. Suffice to say, it seems like a long time ago.

And on my first day in an office, on Guy Fawkes night, the opening gambit of the graduate programme was that leadership was the one thing to which everyone should aspire. We were all to become leaders. Everyone. And we were going to be trained in new skills that meant we would be brilliant at it. And if you weren't a leader, you were a no one. Bring on the fireworks.

Now, I've never done any soldiering, but even back then it seemed to me that if a battalion was full of generals a whole lot of important things would never get done. And through my entire career, sadly, little has changed.

Over the last 30 years I've worked in mining, retail, waste, food, renewable energy, construction, oil & gas, not-for-profit, security, prisons, consulting, telecoms, investment banking and information & analytics. I have led some people, led some teams, led some projects and helped lead big organisations through major crises and massive upheaval.

But mostly I have been a follower. Like everyone else reading these words. Someone who follows their boss, their boss's boss and, ultimately, the company that employs me. I do following 95 percent of my time at work. Never forget, before anything else you are a follower, whether you like the sound of it or not. And the role of followers is to help their leaders, particularly in moments of weakness. My word, did

I say leaders have moments of weakness? God forbid.

So why did no one ever teach me how to be a good follower? Why have none of us ever been on a followership course? And why is there practically nothing written about it? Anywhere. If you search 'followership', you get just over a million results. Try 'leadership' and it's over 2.6 billion. It's a gaping lacuna in organizational theory. I'd like to start the conversation to fill that gap.

If you've got this far and are still interested, then read on. But be warned, it might get a bit uncomfortable.

By now you are probably thinking about sheep

Of course, no one wants to admit they're a follower. It sounds career limiting. Much better to be a global head of something: punctuation, perhaps, for someone like me in the world of communications. Maybe I'll ask.

Just go to LinkedIn, for a laugh, and see how many people inflate their profiles to make themselves sound like global leaders. When they really aren't. All these amazing leaders, but leading who exactly? Imagine how refreshing it might be if we were to read on someone's profile that they were a darn fine follower.

Nothing ever comes of those who follow in an organization. It's the brave heart out front, waving the flag and spouting leadership jargon who gets the glory, right?

So, people clearly feel an overwhelming need to distinguish themselves from those who they perceive as sheep. How uncool to be just a sheep like everyone else. Blindly obeying instructions. Stumbling around on a hillside with no purpose. Just waiting for something or someone to create a sense of urgency and a reason to get moving.

This is the image of a follower that springs from leadership pedagogy. But it's a myth. Fake news of the most damaging kind for any organization.

Great leaders, when we can find them, are only successful because they create an environment where their team can be exceptional followers. As a leader, your best days aren't realized because you did good leading. It's because your people did good following. It's the zenith of narcissism to think otherwise.

So, develop as a leader all you like, but if you don't make good followers along the way, you're doomed. But here's the rub. You can only make good followers of your people by being a good follower yourself.

As the Lord Commander of the Night's Watch, Jeor Mormont, in *Game Of Thrones* said to Jon Snow: 'You want to lead one day? Well learn how to follow.' So, for all of us who don't live in Westeros, this means that if you want to get on at work, you must first learn how to be a good follower.

And I'm not just talking to early career professionals here. It applies to everyone. It applies to you. It is my belief that people's careers top out for no other reason than they stop following or get given such a nice office they don't think it applies to them anymore. If that's you, think again. Who are you following at work and are you any good at it?

A forgotten art

Rediscovering followership means doing some digging. The good news is it's digging inside to remember what you should be doing when you come to work. So, you don't have to look too far.

The uncomfortable truth though is that when we do that soul-searching, we uncover the need for some seemingly unfashionable traits these days such as loyalty, reliability, self-reliance, integrity, poise, perseverance, patience, thoughtfulness, responsiveness, fidelity, optimism, sacrifice and courage. Let me show you.

The best followers turn up no matter what. No matter how hard things get, they stand strong. They believe in their choice of whom to follow because they trust themselves to have made the right choice in the first place. They know what they need to do to keep the faith. They know what they have to put up with sometimes and they know that if they show their support, they can help change things for the better, even if it may take time. Think of the millions on the terraces and in the stadiums each week at sporting events around the world. Well try to remember pre-pandemic at least.

How many people at work think like that? Few. Why? Because they have abdicated responsibility for their initial choice to join that organization. They have drifted into a place where they feel justified in blaming others, usually leaders, for their own lack of success. But instead of either taking responsibility for change or moving on, both of which require courage and self-reliance, they stay and hope that one day they will be the leader and everything will get better.

It's understandable, because it's the path of least emotional resistance. No one likes to think they have made a bad choice and when confronted with the reality that they might have, they go into denial.

But to follow well requires skills, attributes and behaviours that many have forgotten how to use in the workplace, because we have been distracted by the promise of leadership and lured away from the obvious.

Followership means toeing the company line, following the ethical codes, ceasing the moaning, knowing when to challenge your boss – and when not to. It means relying on yourself, doing what you are asked to do, but doing it better than expected. It means thinking about the broader context of your work, sometimes accepting that others know more than you do. It means never talking poorly of others, ending zero-sum games, seeing your boss as an equal and having their back, even if you aren't entirely sure they always have yours. It means seeing colleagues as partners and not as competitors. It means keeping yourself informed, turning up no matter what and doing your best no matter how tough things become. And, it means staying calm in a crisis, being true to yourself, treating people as you would like to be treated and doing the right thing. But above all, it means following your heart.

Never in the history of work could so much be given by so many

On average, based on modern-day spans of control, only about one in eight employees in any large organization is a manager of people or what we might describe in some way as a leader.

So, do we leave the destiny of our workplace entirely to the decisions of so few? Of course not. Let's face it, leadership is what others do to you. Without wanting to sound like a revolutionary in a dodgy beret, isn't it time more of us retook control of our work life by becoming good followers and know that doesn't mean we are subservient to others' whims?

'As a leader, your best days aren't realized because you did good leading. It's because your people did good following. It's the zenith of narcissism to think otherwise.'

Investing in leadership skills would seem important. But wouldn't investing in followership make more sense? Given we know 100 percent of people at work are followers one way or another. All these followers contributing. Imagine the power they would unleash, if they all did it as well as they could?

As Robert Kelley wrote in the *Harvard Business Review* back in 1988 (before even I started work): 'Groups with many leaders can be chaos. Groups with none can be very productive.' Disappointingly, there hasn't been much decent writing on followership since.

I'm not saying that leadership skills aren't important, it's just that they are not as important. Step back for a moment, take a breath and let that thought sink in. The more senior you become, the more honed your followership skills have to be. After all, you are following fewer people and it's much harder to hide. So, if you want to get on, learn how to follow. Which brings us on to the amount of money we invest.

Leadership training is expensive. Very expensive. Upwards of £2000 per person per day is the going rate. It's a demand thing. Everyone wants it, so it's a perpetual race to find the latest approach based on a questionable root in popular or academic psychology. And, when someone comes up with a new thing, the fad spreads like wildfire through the consulting and training community and the costs spiral.

And more worrying still, recent research shows that a whopping 58 percent of leaders out there in the big wide world say they have never received any leadership training. So, I take that to mean that most leaders in the workforce were promoted because they were simply good at what they did and not necessarily good at helping the people around them to be more effective.

Followership, by contrast, is more organic. We already know how to do it. We just forgot. Because we were all too busy trying to be leaders. So, training in followership starts with unlearning the bad habits and modelling those who do it well. It's like copying, only smarter. It means unpacking all those little things that make a difference and making use of them yourself in your own way.

It's worth a ponder, don't you think? After all, how many times are you presented with a chance to get on at work which is wholly within your control?

3. GOBBLEDYGOOK

CORPORATE JARGON IS KILLING MEANING
AND PRODUCTIVITY AT WORK

There are said to be around 300,000 words in the English language of which about 30,000 are in common use for native speakers. Among those 300,000 words, we are blessed with so many glorious synonyms for the word gobbledygook. Gibberish, claptrap, poppycock, balderdash, twaddle, codswallop, hogwash, malarkey, tosh, boloney, flimflam and guff. The list goes on.

So, let's explore the use of corporate gobbledygook. This non-language, this word salad, this idiom insanity that has crept into our work lives and left people mesmerized. And ask where does it come from, why do we use it, what purpose does it serve and what damage does it do?

When the hell did we start talking about kimonos?

The next time you feel the overwhelming desire to 'take it offline', 'not boil an ocean', 'feedforward', 'herd some cats', 'shift a paradigm', 'hold an ideation session' or 'open the kimono', by all means knock yourself out. Just don't use these phrases when doing it.

Firstly, you will, in all probability, sound ridiculous, but more likely you will sound like someone who has just come back from a leadership course. And we all know how welcome that can be.

My theory is someone takes a simple word or action that we do at work, then seeks to elevate its importance, or more likely their own importance, by using a more obscure word that means the same thing or by turning it into a poor excuse for metaphor or idiom. In this way, making improvements becomes 'moving the needle' and doing the easy stuff first becomes 'tackling low hanging fruit'. You can see the allure.

But the recipe for a great metaphor is that it makes the mundane brilliantly different yet truly parallel. It paints a vivid picture or brings an unexpected new insight. A bad metaphor fails to do any of that. And on that definition, in the corporate world, we fail miserably.

As these phrases become substituted for plain English, the long-term effect becomes hypnotic, almost comforting.

And, therefore, induces dreamlike states. That's why poets use metaphors: they eliminate the specific and stifle action. The opposite of what they were intended to do at work. So why do we all play this weird game?

Well, sociology says that if we all use the same language in a community, it helps build identity and a sense of belonging. We feel like we are all in the same tribe. It maybe also gives us a shorthand for our work so we can understand each other quickly.

The dreaded acronym and initialism are also adding fuel to the fire of confusion. If we all know what they stand for, like FYI or CEO, then maybe we can justify their use. But FOMO? I don't have a fear of missing out. I have FOBI, a fear of being included, in the desire to make everything an acronym. I was going to describe all this as bull****, but that's NSFW.

So, at a time when the competition for people's time at work has never been fiercer, what do we do? We speak in ways that over-elaborate, take too long and impart no information. No wonder no one has the capacity to take on anything new.

Maybe that's why there is this constant fight for meaning in the modern world of work and demand for improved productivity. We are simply hypnotizing ourselves out of being able to see meaning or being able to focus on getting the job done. How can people have meaning in what they do if they are focused on 'changing the game with a silver bullet'?

A recipe for exclusion and confusion

'The bus is red' is unquestionably easier to understand than 'the urban passenger transportation vehicle is vermillion in colouration'. In the same way that 'we have to reduce the size of the workforce' is obviously preferable to 'there is a strategic need to rightsize and reallocate resources to business areas where synergies are more effectively realized'. But haven't we all heard the latter, one way or another?

Businesses, and people within them, use this type of weaponized language and obfuscation to mask a harsh reality. They also think that longer words and sentences help show they have thought deeply about it. But employees feel they are being lied to or taken for fools. Surely this is the best example of 'a circle that needs squaring'.

Even as someone who works with language all day long, I am regularly confused by all this. As I had never seen it written down before doing research for this chapter, I thought 'drinking the Kool Aid', meant people were sitting back after a successful piece of work drinking a cold glass of fizzy pop in celebration. When, in fact, it is an expression used to refer to a person who believes in a possibly doomed or dangerous idea because of perceived potential high rewards. The roots of this phrase are truly shocking.

The recent explosion in unintelligible job titles is also to blame. Everyone knows what an accountant does, a doctor, a writer, a pianist, a bricklayer, a lawyer, an auditor or a programmer. But a 'next gen talent acquisition vice president'? An as yet unborn person who buys skills and is also in charge of a woodworking tool, perhaps?

Maybe the solution is if you cannot describe your job in one word then it's probably too confusing for even you to know what it is you are supposed to be doing.

'Never think that corporate jargon makes you sound more intelligent or more important. It does precisely the reverse. When you feel one of these idioms bubbling up, pause and use something a 16-year-old would understand instead.'

Job adverts often start causing problems right from the outset. Saying that you are seeking to hire 'a self-starting, laser-focused, project management ninja who can hit the ground running' is either going to attract those who should be under supervision or put people with any intellect right off even considering your organization. And, even if you were brave enough to put this nonsense aside, imagine joining a new company or team weighed down with such corporate guff. You'd feel excluded from what was going on and your only choice would be to join in.

If native English speakers are left in the dark, spare a thought for colleagues who have English as a second or third language. In workplaces where global working is now commonplace, this just adds to the confusion by excluding people who simply don't understand what is being said or, worse still, infer something entirely different.

After all, doesn't 'let's circle back on this' really mean I don't want to talk about it? Doesn't 'we've decided to pivot' mean we've messed up? And doesn't 'it is what it is' really mean I know I should say something, but right now I can't think what to say? No wonder people are confused.

You might think that this flimflam is the preserve of consultants trying to wow us with just how bright they are and how much value they will add. Probably to justify their exorbitant fees. However, now it seems, we have all been infected with this nonsense. And the prognosis isn't good.

The contagion is real

Some years ago, the organization I worked for at the time asked me to go on a secondment for a few weeks to help with a special project in Scotland. The team I was working with comprised a bunch of specialists from within our own company and those from our partners.

While I was there, I learnt a new word: outwith. It's a Scottish term meaning outside or beyond. As in 'this bit of work falls outwith the scope of the project'. I like learning new words so I put it in my memory bank.

In a later job at a different company I raised the issue of corporate jargon as the business was rife with it and people were struggling to understand what was happening. Or, indeed, what they were expected to do. In fact, there was one colleague who never seemed to use verbs at all when you spoke to him. 'How was the meeting?', I would ask. 'A discourse on synergistic deliverables for ecommerce' would be the response.

So, I decided to do an experiment to see how quickly new phrases or words would spread. I inserted the innocuous 'outwith' into this new company by using it in my conversations and writings. Within three months I was hearing it being played back at me from every corner of this business.

My mischievous experiment proved just how readily people at work pick up new language and add it to their vocabulary. It all seemed normal. But it was highly contagious. A face covering wouldn't stop it and neither would a two metre social distance.

So, what's the harm? In this instance, no harm. But what of the more flowery metaphor-rich phrases we hear every day such as 'thinking outside the box', 'giving 110 percent' or 'getting everyone on the same page'? Does anyone really know what these things mean or what they should do when they hear them?

'Bringing the best version of yourself to work' is one of the latest phrases of meaningless drivel to surface in our workplaces. It's my personal favourite, as I often decide to leave different versions of myself all over the place.

So, don't let it be your keyboard or your mouth using these words. Take a stand against this nonsense and challenge those who use it. As a communicator in business, I have spent much of my working life removing it and every time I do, people breathe a sigh of relief. It's been like blowing out matches before lighting cigarettes. It's difficult, but ultimately you know it's for the best to break the habit.

And don't ever make the mistake of thinking that using corporate jargon makes you sound more intelligent or more important. It does precisely the reverse. When you feel one of these idioms bubbling up inside the queue of words you are about to say, pause and use something a 16-year-old would understand instead. Try it, it's quite refreshing.

Dumbing up

Now, having said all of this, it would be unwise to eliminate all technical language from organizations. I once worked down a mine in Africa. The whole crew was focused on chasing the fuchsitic siliceous dolomite a mile underground. Why? Because that's the rock that contained the gold and if the mine captain caught us referring to it as FSD or any other name, he exploded. He was like a surgeon in his demand for precision as he literally cut the veins of gold from the ground.

If a mining engineer has to have technical words to get the job done, then, of course, so must people in a whole host of other work environments. But we need to learn to recognize the difference between this valuable language and the bunkum that simply fills up corporate airtime.

It's time we let the latter go. Because if we don't, reputations are at stake. Not only our own personal reputations, but the media likes nothing better these days than shaming a company for wheeling out the corporate codswallop.

Maybe less really is more

Let me finish with a recent and quite frightening thought. Tom Whipple, science editor at *The Times*, recently reported on the findings from a study looking at 64,000 dissertations within the academic community under the headline 'Big words are a front for little knowledge'.

In a nutshell, the research showed that the lower the status of the university, the more acronyms and jargon their PhD students used in their theses in an attempt to jostle for recognition. He conclued his piece by saying: 'the preceding dialectic provides a metacontextualization of the academic linguistic gestalt. Or in other words, it suggests that, often, big words are a load of tosh.'

Perhaps we would all do well to consider that if we can't express our idea without buzzwords, maybe there isn't an idea there at all. After all, people who want to be successful use this kind of language. People who are successful, don't. If you would like to make up your own jargon, why not use the Gobbledygook Generator from the Plain English Campaign. You can find it on the web. Literally, minutes of fun.

4. ENGAGEMENT

ENGAGE YOURSELF, DON'T WAIT
FOR IT TO BE DONE TO YOU

Employee engagement. I want to explore exactly what it is, why we hear about it so much, why it matters and what we can learn from it to help our own career journeys.

Employee engagement theory sets out what an organization needs to do to attract people, retain them, develop them and then make sure that they do their best each working day for their colleagues and their customers by aligning every activity with the organizational strategy. Why? Because organizations that effectively engage their people consistently outperform their peers.

However, this simple idea has often become lost in the layers of initiatives that organizations pile onto their people.

I also think we have never really paid enough attention to the power each employee holds to engage themselves, make themselves successful and, thereby, make the organization that employs them successful. So, I want to introduce the idea of self-engagement and to start thinking about it as a tool for career success.

In this chapter we unpack this somewhat murky world of employee engagement and get back to a few, simple ideas that are proven to work.

It all kicked off in the early 1990s

Back in 1994, when I was working at one of the UK's first community-wide recycling centres and the Channel Tunnel linking the UK and France first opened, *Harvard Business Review* quietly published a transformational paper about a new concept called the Service Profit Chain.

The editor describes it as a 'simple, elegant, and ultimately tough-minded way to build profitability in a service business. It offers as much today as it did then and is a perennial bestseller'.

In a nutshell, this article, for the first time, set out overwhelming evidence that if you provide excellent internal service to your employees, you will be better placed to improve what they then called employee satisfaction, which then drives retention and enhanced productivity. This, in turn, generates value for customers, so building customer loyalty, revenue growth and profitability. The organization then has the resources to reinvest in further improvements to internal service quality. And so, the virtuous cycle continues.

For me, this is the birth of employee engagement, although we didn't call it that until much more recently, and at the time I was too busy working out mechanical techniques for separation of mixed household waste to notice.

'If you cannot see how your tasks further the cause of the business, you should ask to be shown and if you are still not convinced, then you should stop doing them.'

Nearly 30 years on, employee engagement has become a thing. It's real, recognized, valued and organizations invest heavily to improve it, often having people who are solely responsible for it.

In our modern world of work there is an undeniable logic to this model. Our instincts and everyday experiences in the workplace tell us this way of doing things must be true. It has, to a certain extent, become normalized. And that is testament to the robustness of the initial research.

But, sadly, this doesn't mean that organizations know how to implement it properly. Employee engagement remains something most organizations are striving to achieve. For many, it remains elusive, not least because employee expectations are changing all the time and just when you think you have hit the target, it has moved.

The modern engagement story

Employee engagement today, in its simplest terms, describes the relationship between an organization and its people. An engaged employee is seen as someone who is enthusiastic about their work and their employer and one who takes positive action to further the organization's interests, reputation and performance, knowing that these actions will, ultimately, be of benefit to them as individuals. By definition, a disengaged employee is one who at best coasts or at worst causes disruption.

At the next level beyond actions, we start to think about values, the things that drive behaviour. Engaged employees invariably share the same values as their employer. The motivations to do good work are born from the fact that employees care about their work because their employer cares about the same things as they do. There is a common cause.

In practice this means engaged employees will, among other things, innovate more, take better care of assets, mitigate risk, look after customers well, be more productive, follow safety practices, stay longer and manage others effectively. And, the ultimate prize, they will become advocates for their organization, boosting the brand and recommending good people to join. Who doesn't want people like that around?

Does that sound like you? If not, then roll up your sleeves and get busy. Unless you have the time or inclination to wait around for someone to do something for you.

On this point about employee referrals, we need to explore why it matters so much. Recent research shows that referred employees have much higher conversion rates on application, their retention rates are higher and so are their engagement and, in turn, advocacy rates. People like people like themselves, so an organization's diverse people recommending their friends often leads to more good people joining. And the whole hiring cost, which can be expensive when agencies are involved, is much reduced. What's not to like?

So, engaged employees are good to have. Disengaged, not so much. Which is why organizations are focused on it. The organization then rewards these people, not because they are engaged *per se*, but because they repeatedly make good things happen.

Engagement in what exactly?

But at this point to provide some specificity and useful guidance we must ask the question, engagement in what, exactly?

My years of experience in this field tell me that it starts and ends with an employee understanding their organization's strategy and making sure that they know what actions they need to take to drive it. This applies to every single employee, no matter what their role. It applies to you. If you cannot see how your tasks further the cause of the business, you should ask to be shown and, if you are still not convinced, then you should stop doing them.

Many of us will have heard the perhaps apocryphal story of the cleaner at NASA in the 1960s, who, when asked what their job was, responded by saying that they were helping to put people on the moon. If this is true, then we might say that this person was the model of an engaged employee who understood and was motivated by their employer's higher purpose. My question to you is what is your 'putting people on the moon moment'? Because finding that and being motivated by it will be your sustaining nourishment through every trial and tribulation, we all inevitably face at one time or another.

Engaging employees in the strategy and higher purpose, so they feel personally implicated in its success is the single most effective thing an organization can do by way of engagement. And I am sorry to say that everything else is tinsel by comparison.

Let me give you an example. Through my time at work, I have heard much talk about internal customers. Let me tell you, no one has internal customers. We may have colleagues with whom we must work productively and for whom we must provide great service. But customers are the ones paying for the product or service. Many people in corporate functions lose sight of this and think, mistakenly, that if they provide good service to their internal customers then their responsibility is done. It isn't. They must do both: provide great service to their colleagues with a clear understanding of how this benefits the paying customer. Without that knowledge, they are not properly aligned to the organizational strategy or the improved performance of the organization. The Service Profit Chain tells us this.

If you look around you, it is my assertion that you will

see many similar such examples every day, all conspiring to tear you away from your direct link to driving strategy. It's not deliberate, it's just organizations tend to forget how important that link is and inadvertently put stuff in the way.

Before we leave this section, I want to address a couple of issues on nomenclature and semantics for the linguistic pedants among you.

Satisfaction in the context we are discussing here is not the same as engagement, although often the words get used in the same breath. Some may seek my defenestration for saying so, but satisfaction matters not one iota at work. It is completely possible to be totally satisfied but utterly disengaged. We've all met these people, usually buried somewhere in the background, just doing their thing year in year out, preferring to be left alone, never challenging anything, never making suggestions, the kind of people who pick up their pay cheque each month but actually left years ago. In fact, the word 'satisfied' implies passivity at work. Who wants to just be satisfied? We spend so much time working shouldn't we demand much more than that?

I also want to mention a relatively new term that we are sure to be hearing a lot more about in the coming years and that is 'employee experience': the idea that engagement is won or lost at all the touchpoints through an employee journey, physical, cultural and technological. I will leave you to explore this latest piece of management theory should you so wish, but if we are agreed that alignment with strategy is the golden thread of engagement, then employee experience is just one of many supporting acts.

Ultimately, the power rests with you

So, focusing now on the subtitle of this chapter, I want to explore what power we each have as employees over our own engagement. Organizations are focused on doing it to their people, when it seems to me that the real power comes when we take it upon ourselves to self-engage. After all, by self-engaging we can take back control of our own destiny by using a proven model in ways that are sustainable for us.

Imagine, for a moment, working for an organization whose values are different from yours. The organization, for example, cares about and rewards speed, bravery, risk-taking and profit. Your values are more aligned to ethical working, inclusion, sustainable performance and community.

Of course, you might say this would never happen given such divergence. But it does. It happens a lot in the workplace, because these things get missed out in the recruitment process or one side or both convince themselves other things matter more.

Then one day, to better engage you, you are subjected to the dreaded change programme that aims to inculcate you, and everyone else, with the organization's values. At which point the psychological contract between employee and employer inevitably starts to fray. How could it not?

I worked for a company that decided to introduce some new values. These weren't derived from any kind of employee involvement or consultation. They were decided upon by a marketing team. One of the values was bravery. It's a good value on the face of it, but all that happened was every employee was given a postcard with it written in big gold letters. And then nothing. People were confused at first, then angry. What were they supposed to do with it? Weren't they brave already? A real opportunity wasted.

Having values imposed on you can be a desperately uncomfortable and even damaging place to be in any walk of life. At work, it can quickly build disenfranchisement and resentment.

This is an extreme example to make the point but unwritten psychological contracts are made through all sorts of things such as the recruitment process, opportunities for growth, the behaviours of line managers and leaders, the way in which the organization communicates with you, how you are rewarded and how you are treated when you decide to leave. It's a long list of those touchpoints we talked about earlier. But the cause of disengagement, in my experience, is usually far simpler than this.

Someone once told me that people join an organization but leave their line manager. I'll let you ponder this thought for yourselves, as to its veracity. But what I would say is that a line manager's poor behaviour or performance will disengage you faster than pretty much anything else. So, what to do if this is where we find ourselves and I imagine many do?

You joined your organization, hopefully, because at some level you supported its purpose and found it inspiring and motivational, however hard it may have been to see how your role would directly support it. If you feel disengaged, then you should revisit your original motivations and recognize that the higher purpose is bigger than any obstacles you will invariably find at work, including a dysfunctional line manager.

However, if your higher purpose for coming to work is not enough to sustain you through challenging times, then you need to make sure you deploy your best followership skills to help see you through. And, if that fails, then you should think about moving on. We rarely talk about leaving an organization as being okay, but it is a positive action which should be celebrated as a valid and proactive choice if all else fails.

So, in best followership tradition, engaging yourself means looking for that all-important link between what you do and your organization's strategy. I know it can sometimes be hard to find, especially in super-sized organizations, but find it you must.

It means looking for opportunities to align your values with those of your employer. To find your values, spend some time thinking about the things that matter most to you in life and keep asking yourself why they matter. And then ask why again, until you get to single words. Hopefully your organization has clearly articulated values. If it doesn't, ask why not. After all, values help organizations and people to make decisions. How can they make good decisions if they don't know what they value?

Self-engagement also means understanding policy and procedure and following them. It doesn't mean relinquishing your enquiring mind or simply accepting the status quo. But there will always be rules and you should know what they are and what your role is in following them.

It also means speaking up when things don't feel right and understanding the risks to which your organization is exposed and doing your bit to mitigate them. These aren't solely the responsibilities of senior leaders or risk management professionals. They are yours too.

Engaging yourself means supporting the corporate

responsibility efforts of your employer and playing your part to support the communities in which you operate. It means doing what you can to include yourself in the fabric of the organization and looking for ways to progress by deploying your skills and experiences.

It means taking good care of your work-life balance and, ultimately, it means looking for ways for you to become an advocate of your organization. What would have to be true for you to say to your best friend that where you work is simply superb and you would have no hesitation in recommending it as a good place to work?

In short, self-engagement means taking back control of all the key areas of employee engagement on your own terms and at your own speed. And ideally faster than perhaps everyone around you might expect.

5. CULTURE

LANGUAGE, SYMBOLS, TRADITIONS AND
NORMS SHAPE YOUR PERFORMANCE

Organizations have distinct cultures, plural, whether they manage them or not. Whether they can articulate them or not. Organizations of any scale that say they have a single culture are, in my experience, often deluding themselves. It's more of a wish than a reality.

Micro-cultures dominate. And while sometimes they may feel similar. Often, they don't.

Culture is simply the answer to the question: what's it like to work around here? Depending on who you ask in any given organization and where, the specific answers are sure to be different.

Some will focus on how leaders behave or ethics, others on opportunities for learning or inclusion. Some will talk about team dynamics or innovation, while others will talk about customers or reputation. The list is long.

But more than this, all organizations have a rich soup of language, metaphor, symbols, traditions and norms which have a far more striking, immediate and lasting effect on culture. Whether macro or micro.

Every behaviour, decision, system, policy and process is shaped by this soup in which they sit. And so, in turn, is the organizational performance. Culture matters.

So, let's explore the complexity that is culture and unpack it into its smaller, constituent parts so it's easier to understand, giving you something more malleable with which you can work. Because you will need to work with it one way or another, no matter what your role. When things don't go the way they are supposed to at work, it's usually something in the culture that's broken.

Let's do some unpacking

A culture manifests itself through shared behaviours driven by shared values, even if they are unhealthy ones. Rarely does any organization have a single culture. Although few would admit to that.

Having spoken to senior leaders over many years about organizational culture one consistent theme has emerged.

Their attention span for discussing it is short.

Why? Because it's too nebulous a subject with too many unknowns, too many human variables and too subjective in nature. It's difficult to get a hold of and what would you do even if you did have a firm grip?

So, how do we talk about culture in a way that is meaningful, relevant and useful? The best way I have found is not to talk about it at all. Rather, break it down into its tangible, constituent parts, then talk about those instead.

You'll have more joy because many of these will be on the list of what leaders care most about: vision and values; articulation of strategy; beliefs and behaviours; recruitment and induction; learning and development; performance management; reward and recognition; corporate responsibility, reputation and brand; product or service delivery; working environment; leadership practices; organizational structure, systems, policy and process; compliance and ethics; and technology.

'When things don't go the way they are supposed to at work, it's usually something in the culture that's broken.'

If culture is blamed for something not working, which it often is, you can investigate which constituent part or parts aren't working then you will have something upon which to focus your efforts. You will then know which levers to pull to achieve the changes you want to see. Let me give you three examples.

Exorcising ghosts

I once worked for an organization that had outgrown its office space. It had been there a long time. Expansion and numerous acquisitions had meant much jiggery pokery to fit new people in. The estates team were running around trying to keep everyone happy. And failing.

There were also ghosts. Not the unearthly kind, but the work history kind. Spooky, nonetheless.

Those already present in the building saw new people coming in as an unwelcome invasion. Those moving in from acquisitions saw it as conquering new territory. But some felt like imposters. And these adversarial metaphors ran deeper as time passed. Integration, harmony and productivity were being frustrated.

It was clear that the office environment was central to the problem. A fresh start was needed for everyone. So, a new location was found and planning started to create a new office environment fit for this growing company. Six months later, over a few days, several thousand people were moved to the new office.

The transformation was instant. I have never seen behaviours change so fast, before or since. The old language of them and us fell away, parity was created. People voluntarily shared spaces where before they had not. People looked happier. People socialized. Performance stepped up.

Who knew that one's working environment would turn out to be such a massive lever for change? That's why it makes my list.

One plus one equals three

My second example is about two departments with several hundred people coming together to improve efficiency. Both provided services to customers. But in different ways and different geographies. The business decided that forming a new, co-ordinated approach was the most logical thing to do to improve efficiency, customer service and performance.

One of these teams was renowned for providing stellar customer service. It was culturally ingrained. The other, not so much. This was also culturally ingrained. Not that they wished for it, but it surfaced nonetheless as no one did anything much to counter it.

As an aside, when we asked leaders in each department to come up with a celebrity whom they thought epitomized and characterized their team, the answers were fascinating. I won't use their names here, but one department described itself as a mature, intelligent, successful, female actress who had become part of the fabric of society, was loved by many, captivating and well regarded by critics. The other described itself as a young, hard-hitting, hard-drinking sportsman, known for speaking their mind, playing hard but partying harder, who would often find themselves the subject of unflattering headlines on the back pages. This was going to be an interesting coming together.

In making these two departments one, this cultural difference of attitude towards customers was the biggest challenge. But the solution was truly elegant.

We decided that the only way for employees to value the provision of great service to customers, and thereby do it well, was to provide exemplary internal service to them as employees. We have met the Harvard service chain earlier in this book but here it is again, weaving its magic.

Every internal system, policy and process was overhauled to ensure that great service, internal and external, was top of the agenda and met agreed performance standards. Now when you submitted your expenses, instead of it taking three or four weeks to get your money, or when someone in finance got around to it, it took two days. And always two days. And this ethic extended to any internal service measure you chose to investigate. Great internal service was the priority.

People received excellent internal service and so were far more motivated to give it to their customers. And that's why systems, policy and process also make my list.

No place to hide

My third example is around the use of technology. In my area of work, employee communication, there has been talk for years, decades even, of how technology would irrevocably change and improve the way people inside organizations would communicate, share knowledge, collaborate and engage.

Internal communicators and their technology partners the world over made a slow start in bringing these changes to life, that's for sure. And it has been a slow creep forward since, with organizations lagging way behind in their development of the kind of consumer-grade technologies deployed on the social media platforms we all now take for granted. So much so that they have, in recent years, given up the battle and now simply use these established platforms instead to speak to their own people. Social media platforms have become surrogate internal communication channels.

The lines between internal and external communication have been smudged, so much so that for all intents and purposes they no longer exist. And a good job too.

This has had the effect of opening organizational cultures up to external scrutiny like never before. Corporate websites may still convey messages organizations want their audiences to hear, but social media lets employees, customers, investors and other stakeholders have their say too. There's no place to hide any longer.

For candidates, it has been transformational in being able to get the measure of their potential employer and employees being able to talk about their own employment experiences. Organizational cultures are laid bare, stories of poor behaviours exposed and stories of successes shared with the kind of reach that the brave can harness but will terrify the weak. And organizational cultures are improving as a result. It is just the start of the power technology can bring. So, technology makes the list.

Hopefully, you can see from just these three examples that if you want to succeed at work you need to pay close attention to the drivers of culture. Not only for your own sanity and ultimate benefit but that of your organization.

When the soup is out of date

I look back at one of my previous experiences with a wry smile. A team of people beset by fiascos. Driven by a dysfunctional micro-culture that was subtle and destructive all in one. The language, metaphors, symbols, traditions and norms were infected with I win, you lose. This was a micro-culture of formidable power. And one that, sadly, I have seen more than once.

The quality of your clothes, the type of car you drove, how old you were, whether you had an office or not, how much you earnt, who you knew, where you went on holiday, whether you were attractive or not. These were the issues that mattered.

Largely image driven, it permeated the whole decision-making process. People playing this game were unable to accept difference or new thought, they found it hard to collaborate, couldn't deal with ambiguity, were uneasy with new people and never admitted mistakes. These things had become cultural norms. Weirdly, my boss was new to this organization too and I saw them become infected before my very eyes.

Differences were highlighted and every opportunity for one-upmanship was exploited. It was the only way of being noticed. You could either join in or be excluded from the gang. You could accept the sobriquet you were given or remain an outsider.

At first, I thought it was risible. It became uncomfortable. Then toxic. This was the culture. And to my mind an almost unfixable one.

No one decided that was how it was going to be. The people had simply stumbled around until they found something, however hideous, that bound them together. Better to have something than nothing with which to identify. People do that. It's quite natural.

This couldn't be fixed by an intervention as in my other examples. This was like an incurable disease. And, this is why I want you to think carefully about your own language, metaphors, symbols, traditions and norms. Building up over time, they can become immensely powerful drivers of success but, as we have seen, can also become a worthy adversary to any form of change.

Thankfully, such bad behaviour is becoming less common in the workplace as we wake up to the power of dignity, humility and compassion. But many of us will have experienced some bad behaviour of one form or another driven by such micro-cultures. The kind of behaviour that eats away at self-confidence. When it exists, it's usually a glitch in the culture that allows it or even, inadvertently, encourages it to happen.

So, understanding the nuances of your organizational culture matters a great deal for success of individuals and of an enterprise. And these nuances are, in my experience, not only found in the overt systems and processes we talked about earlier which are easier to fix, but lurk in the language, metaphors, symbols, traditions and norms, which aren't. For good or for evil.

6. INFLUENCING

THERE IS A RECIPE FOR INFLUENCING
WITHOUT AUTHORITY

I'm willing to place a bet that your most frustrating days at work come to pass because people with whom you work simply don't get what you are trying to do. You have trouble bringing them round to your way of thinking, persuading them to change tack or adopt your new idea. Sound familiar?

If so, you are suffering what many now call an inability to influence without authority. I prefer to think of it as simply struggling to influence others. It's a difficult thing to do in any walk of life. But working in matrices, collaborating with others in different work areas and the need for quick results only serve to exacerbate the problem.

So, how do you sway people's opinions, shape their

thinking to be in line with yours and induce them to agree and take the action you want? It's a tricky business but there is a recipe I have learnt that has proved successful over the years: some practical tools that if you are prepared to invest the time and put in the thinking can deliver results.

'Invest the time to meet others in their world, rather than expecting them to come to yours, by seeking to understand their motivations, beliefs, values, skills, assumptions and their reality.'

It's not easy to persuade a prime minister to endorse a not-for-profit out of the myriad requests they receive. It's even harder to coax a chief executive of a newly merged business to fundamentally change their tone of voice so they create a climate of unity. It also takes some skill to encourage a human resources team to adopt a whole new approach to leadership development.

I want to focus on how you too can go about exercising your influence without any formal seniority. After all, if you must resort to hierarchical authority, if you have it, then some would say you have already failed.

People have called such influencing the 'art of woo'. I really like the sound of that. It's probably the only time it's okay to use this word at work. So here goes.

Our recipe starts with being good at what you do

'Whatever you are, be a good one.'

Abraham Lincoln

Being good at what you do is your start point in being able to influence others. Unless you simply adopt the ideas outlined in the rest of this chapter and become a charlatan. I guess we've all met one or two of those in our time.

I used to have a line manager who schmoozed his way through life. But he would take my work and that of other people, remove our names and present it as his own, not that I knew until much later. He was highly successful for a year or so. Then, inevitably, he got caught out. His career never quite recovered.

Anyway, back to my point. You need to hone your skills in your chosen area and show others that you are a stand-out performer. From here, it is my experience that all the other influencing challenges become much easier.

People tend to respect and trust competence. You'll struggle to influence anyone without first having gained their trust. Trust starts with people seeing you as a safe pair of hands, someone who knows their stuff on whom they can rely to have good judgement and make good things happen. So, whatever you do, don't be the best kept secret in your organization.

It's all very well for me to say become good at what you do. How you do that will vary greatly depending on your chosen career. But there is one gem I can share that will help accelerate your excellence, no matter what your job. And that is modelling people you admire. Let me show you by way of a short story.

I have always found interviewing people for a job difficult and stressful. You only have an hour or so, in which to not only make a judgement about the suitability of the candidate for a role and organization, but also to put on a good enough show so that they have the information they need to be able to make the right choice for them.

Aren't the top three choices we ever make in our lives something like choosing a partner, choosing a house, then choosing a job? And we are all supposed to make the right choice for the third one in only one or two meetings. How long does it normally take us to choose the other things I mentioned?

One day though, I learnt something new. I interviewed for a company with a global leader in their field. And I don't use those words lightly. I was expecting to have the grilling of my life on my work experience. But what did he ask me when we sat down? 'Tell me about where you grew up.'

Initially thrown, I gathered my thoughts and we went on to have a deeply personal conversation for an hour. I got to know him and he got to know me. Choosing each other was easy after that.

I have modelled the way this leader asked questions ever since. And I am happy to report that it has paid dividends. And selecting the right candidate in interviews has become easier too.

Modelling isn't copying. It's deeper than that. The basic premise is that if someone can do something then anyone can. It is concerned with the how, rather than the what or the why. Young children are exceptional modellers of other people. It's just that as we get older, we forget how to do it.

The tricky thing is that you can't just ask someone you admire how they do what they do, as they may not even be aware of it themselves. So, you must deploy your best observation and listening skills, without coming across as a stalker, to see if you can illicit their conscious and unconscious strategies and apply them in your own way to your work.

How do they hold themselves? How do they move their body? Where do they look when they speak? Where do they look when you speak? What tone and pace do they have? What stories do they tell? What kinds of language do they use? What is their desk or office like? The list goes on, but hopefully this gives you some ideas to start. But be warned, patience is required.

Then add a healthy dollop of rapport

Cicero said: 'If you want to persuade me, you must think my thoughts, feel my feelings and speak my words'. In other words, you must almost become the other person. Get inside their head, feel what they feel and walk in their shoes in order to change their perspective. This is a 2000 year-old insight. And nothing has changed today.

It means building rapport: a harmonious, productive and healthy relationship of equals. It's one of those things, rapport, we tend not to think about it when it's working, but we notice in a second when it's gone or if it isn't present. Sounds like that trust word again doesn't it?

Building rapport requires an investment in your audience and knowing who the opinion-formers are. Then focusing on the audience of one, treating people as individuals rather than starting to generalize about certain groups. Your unconscious bias, and we all have some, will scupper you if you go down that route. For me, building rapport starts by paying genuinely close attention to what people say, what they do and how they feel. Let me give you an example of this in action.

I recently decided to buy a new car. I had chosen the brand I wanted but not the type of car. There were several options I liked. I was greeted by a sales representative at the showroom and given a cup of coffee and asked to have a wander around. He'd be with me in a minute.

After a while he returned and asked me what I was looking for. 'Something comfortable but fast', I said. 'A long-legged cruiser that has a luxurious but sporty feel. A great sounding engine is also important, as I haven't quite made the jump to electric yet. I also want something that's airy, light and spacious.' He seemed confused.

He motioned me over to one of the cars and said. 'Take a look at this, beautiful isn't it? Stunning shape, a range of vibrant colours and the latest design. I can really see you in this one.' And so it went on.

We can see already that our language was mismatching. The way we think about cars is completely different. I'm all about feel and sound. He's all visual. The conversation seems awkward now and the chance to build rapport is slipping away. I'm not going to spend that much money with someone I don't trust to understand my needs.

I change tack and go visual in my language. 'Can he show

me what it looks like inside?' 'Can I see the specification for the engine?' 'What might a discount look like?' Rapport builds, trust builds, we get on like a house on fire and I walk away with the best car I have ever owned. And at a healthy discount. He was right, it really is a beauty.

For me, language is probably the most important part of your influencing armoury. If you want to persuade people, listen out for the clues they leave you when they speak, then paint pictures, invoke symphonies or conjure emotions to hit the right spot and never underestimate the power of a good metaphor.

Do this well and you will build relationships and resources around you, then you will find yourself plugged into the heart of what's going on in your organization. This is gold dust.

It's our flexibility to adopt new styles with new people that means we will have the best chance of building rapport and achieving mutually beneficial outcomes. Invest the time to meet others in their world, rather than expecting them to come to yours, by seeking to understand their motivations, beliefs, values, skills, assumptions and their reality. Then try learning something about them that you find genuinely interesting, so you, in turn, seem genuinely interested in them.

I have a reputation for being able to get on with people at

work whom many other people find difficult. It's all down to being able to build rapport.

Finally add a pinch of data to taste

A long and productive stint in a global information and analytics business has taught me many things but the most valuable is the power of data and its ability to drive extraordinary innovation. For my part, I have always liked numbers as well as words, so I have always been keen to show the value of what I do by linking it to the kinds of data that so often resonate with decision-makers in large organizations.

Bringing in data as a convincer also has the effect of bringing in context. In different parts of the world, we see distinct preferences for high or low context. Some cultures want to know all the details and the back story. Others just want to know what you plan to do, when and precious little else. But it is my experience that if people are to be influenced, they all want a broader context to show that the implications of new ideas or changes have been properly thought through. That's why, increasingly, we see decisions by consensus and consultation. It helps bring in broader perspectives and reduces risk.

One of my most productive and successful years at work was driven by powerful and insightful data. I looked in detail at an employee opinion survey which revealed one specific part of employee engagement that was somewhat in need of fixing. This part was employee advocacy or the propensity of employees to recommend their employer as a good place to work. Improving engagement and advocacy has many knock-on benefits in terms of customer service, productivity, performance, compliance, innovation, safety and recruitment. It's a strategic target worth hitting.

I built a strategy around this one data point and showed how by telling human interest stories and showcasing employees in user-generated video that we would be able to improve the advocacy scores.

So, we set about a year-long campaign which broke all records in terms of engagement by any measure we chose to investigate. At the end of the year, employee advocacy scores were tracked again, along with employee referral rates and we had made unprecedented positive strides. This work formed a central part of an award-winning, global approach which ran for several years and kept on delivering.

The lesson here is finding a diamond in the data can go a long way to not only make the case for change but also to prove that you have arrived at the end. Ta-da! By the way, I never use exclamation marks in my writing, and neither should you. No one speaks in exclamation marks. There is only one exception, however, and that is after the word I've just used.

One final thought before I set you off being excellent at work and honing your influencing skills. The addition of a pinch of data also helps you, and your audience, get to grips with the age-old conundrum of what is important and urgent, what is one but not the other and what is neither. Often, I find that people conflate urgency and importance, which can mean getting them onside becomes more difficult. Data help to make the case for prioritization and this can yield dividends in your influencing campaign, especially when people are busy. And who isn't busy these days?

This now brings us to the end of the recipe for woo. I hope it has provided some food for thought.

7. CRISES

YOUR NEXT CRISIS IS NEVER FAR AWAY

The pages of corporate history are littered with poorly managed crises, shattered reputations, financial ruin, environmental catastrophes and media humiliation. Some brought about by an organization's own failings and others by external factors beyond anyone's control. I need not cite them here. We've all read the stories and looked on in amazement at how badly they have been handled. But deep down knowing we probably could have done no better and secretly glad it wasn't happening to us.

These falls from grace have never surprised me though. They're probably the toughest days of anyone's working life to be in the eye of such a storm and often crises move so fast it's nigh on impossible to keep ahead of them. That has been my own experience through a not insignificant number of crises that have darkened many a day during my career.

I think it's perhaps just the nature of this particular beast in the modern world of work. Managing a crisis is hard to get right because we can never be truly prepared, social media adds a fury that's hard to navigate and each major incident is never like the last.

It seems to me though that there's a degree of inevitability about being hit by a crisis. Part of me thinks it's even all perfectly normal. It's how you handle them that counts. An employee messes up by accident or design, systems fail, a terrorist strikes or nature steps in to tear things apart. Large and small, I have lost count of the number of crises I have been involved in over the last 30 years.

Being a communications professional, my reflections here are undoubtedly titled towards my own experiences and research I have done in that field. But isn't it true that effective communication is always at the heart of managing a crisis well?

So, before we begin, we need to ask ourselves how many of us are even slightly prepared? What are the procedures, who is responsible for doing what and will your business continuity plan, assuming you have one, stand up to the extreme buffeting of something truly testing and unexpected?

It's not a priority, until it's a priority

It is my observation that at a human level, we are not well equipped to prepare properly for things which may or may not happen. In our everyday working lives, there are simply too many other priorities to spend much time preparing for a what-if.

While I am sure we all accept that our business continuity teams have a job to do, it seems to me that people find it all slightly frustrating that we must spend time building plans and reviewing them each year. Just in case. All too often the co-ordinator of such plans is a junior team member. Doesn't that tell us something about the value we place on preparedness?

I worked for an organization that went through a routine, mini crisis at one of its offices. A chemical leak closed the building without notice for two days. We found out late one evening so we emailed all colleagues and told them to work at home or go to one of our other locations nearby. Each employee had a company laptop so they could work anywhere, but it turned out that nearly two-thirds of them never took theirs home, which resulted in anger, chaos and much lost work on the first day.

The organization might have had robust workarounds in place for such an eventuality, but no one had paid any attention, thinking they would never be needed. When we asked people after the event why they didn't routinely take their laptops home they said it was because they lived so close to the office it wasn't necessary. They also said, because they lived so far away, they weren't prepared to carry it.

One of the responders also said we had over-engineered this whole thing following what was essentially a once-in-a-lifetime event. A month later, there was a fire in the dry cleaners next door.

Only after this second disruption did people start to get the message. It usually takes something big to hit for an organization to take preparedness seriously. They have to go through the wringer and feel the pain. After that, the plans make sense. That's when time is invested in rehearsals and, most importantly, that's when crisis preparedness stays on the management agenda.

Someone once told me that to see a yellow car you have to own a yellow car. And once you do, you see them everywhere. It's the same with a crisis. Once you have experienced one, then you are much better placed to see the next one coming. It's a shame we all must learn the hard way. But it seems this is just the way it is.

You can't get a masters in crisisology

Unfortunately, you cannot study how to truly manage any given crisis well. You must learn through experience and treasure your learning, as it will be all you have to prepare you for the next one. However, no matter how wild your imagination, you will probably face challenges neither you nor anyone else could ever have foreseen. Take my own experiences for example.

I escaped with my life following a mining accident. Explosives were detonated in a tunnel without the required warnings. I wasn't too far away. Not so much a corporate crisis but a personal one. But perhaps I should have known this was the start of a trend.

An ordinary day was turned on its head when a full-size, wind-tunnel model of a surface-to-air naval missile turned up in a lorry carrying waste at a processing site that I managed. Not that at the time anyone knew it was a model, so this resulted in the partial evacuation of the local town and the mobilization of bomb disposal and ordinance experts from the military. And my first foray into the world of dealing with the media when things go wrong. I think they call that a baptism of fire.

It seems I was pretty good in a crisis, so I was asked to move into corporate communications. Then, as a newly appointed communications manager, I had to deal with employees using heavy machinery who had been drugged with the milk in their coffee being laced with LSD by a former, disgruntled colleague.

A year or so later, one of my colleagues was arrested for unwittingly aiding an attempted contract killing. One of this colleague's workmates was arranging to have a hitman take out his wife's lover. Unknowingly, they wrote and posted the letter arranging a meeting which turned out to be the planned hit.

'A crisis is never far away for any of us ... we should each expect to have to deal with one every three years or so while at work.'

A couple of years later, several employees were tragically killed in a helicopter accident. My role was to keep the media away from the families, at a time when all they wanted to do was precisely the opposite and celebrate the lives of their lost heroes.

My next crisis was to deal with a group of environmental activist shareholders, who each bought a single share, pitched up and decided to start throwing chairs at the chair, during an annual general meeting I helped organize. I have been to some interesting AGMs in my time but this one took the biscuit.

I was honing my crisis skills by this point, but nothing prepared me for the naked aggression of animal rights protestors who turned up outside head office and started attacking employees as they arrived.

Then an absent-minded employee in a digger cut through cables during a football World Cup, killing coverage of a crucial England game for hundreds of thousands of viewers.

Like many of us, the 2008 financial meltdown and subsequent sovereign debt crisis in Europe presented all sorts of challenges, but I was working in banking at the time and was right in the thick of it.

I was with a Japanese company when the devastating 2011 Tōhoku tsunami made landfall. And finally, like everyone else reading this book, Covid-19. The ultimately predictable pandemic for which no one, anywhere, was properly prepared despite stark warnings for many years. Didn't I say as humans we don't like wasting time on what-ifs?

I have often wondered if, somehow, I was a magnet for a crisis. The truth is one is never far away for any of us. I have been working for 30 years or so. Assuming I am not jinxed, given the eleven big ones I can recall above, we should each expect to have to deal with a crisis of one sort or another every three years or so while at work. And you don't have to work in management, communications, health and safety, or business continuity to be prepared. If I have learned one thing, it's that you can never know what kind of crisis may hit and it could be your turn next time to be in the eye of the storm, no matter what your role.

The three lessons

So, what have I learned through all these different crises that I can share with you? To give you a fast start in thinking about crisis management in your own work, here are three lessons I can draw from my own experiences.

Living with unpredictability

Crises tend to come out of nowhere. Some might be more predictable than others in your sector or industry, but how they play out rarely follows any pattern. You can't know what is around the corner, but you can be sure of one thing. It won't be anything like business as usual.

However, despite this, time is well spent thinking about your primary organizational risks. If your company produces an annual report, these will be clearly set out along with mitigation. If they are worth their salt, your risk management professionals will have thought deeply about these risks, consulting widely inside and outside your organization. These pre-identified risks are a good place to start planning for what you would do in your work area if one were to materialize.

It might then be worth having a brainstorm to see what else could crop up. Think the unimaginable for a moment and see where it takes you. You might be surprised.

This thinking time will not be wasted. At least you will start to pay attention to the roles, responsibilities, systems and processes that will need to work well to manage your worst-case scenarios. These are always your first steps, even if you cannot with any surety predict the exact nature of the event that will trigger their use.

Rehearse your response

The most effective way to prepare for a crisis, or even prevent one, is to rehearse one. I don't mean a desk rehearsal. I mean a real one with crisis plans invoked. Teams come together to work through a presented scenario, pulling in business continuity, health and safety, technology, human resources, real estate, legal, finance, operations, communications and all the key departments, co-ordinated by your incident management team which is fully up and running.

This approach is designed to help you plan your way out of issues before you must face them for real, testing your approach in a safe environment and not in the inevitable chaos of a real crisis. A good rehearsal may well flag issues so important that the process actually helps you prevent a crisis in the first place.

Rehearsing also helps you identify those people in your organization who cope and those who don't. Some people adapt more quickly and can apply their experiences to challenging new situations more easily than others. Crises tend to make or break people. It's better to know who your stars are ahead of time. You never know where the solution to a work crisis might come from, so working closely with flexible thinkers will always stand you in good stead.

Rehearsing also brings about a shift in your organizational state of mind. It shows your people and your customers that you care enough to invest the effort and that you are not complacent, even when things are going well. It shows the kind of forethought and prudence we rarely see in these fire-fighting days.

So, accept that you will be subject to crises and do your preparation to make sure you are one of those people who is made by one, not broken by one.

Find the right leader

You must seek out those who have the experience or the natural skills to lead during a crisis. It could well be that these are not the most senior people. When the pressure is truly on in the cauldron of a major incident, some people simply become overwhelmed.

If it is obvious to everyone concerned that your organization has messed up, your spokesperson (yes, you should only have one) has to say so, apologize and set out what will be done to fix it. The lawyers will often advise otherwise but this just adds to the pressure of a cooker waiting to explode.

If your organization wasn't responsible, you can still apologize for the impact of any events on your customers, employees and other stakeholders. Showing people that you care and have their best interests at heart will buy you valuable time.

In the immediate aftermath of the helicopter crash in which I was involved, it didn't matter who or what was responsible. What mattered was getting support for the families of the colleagues who had lost their lives. I have never seen a work community come together so quickly to do just that, with such compassion and a determination to be by their side and help at every step.

You must do all you can to get ahead of the story, regularly communicating with internal and external audiences to keep them informed of developments, even if there is no solution as yet. But don't forget, you do need a solution. You must fix what went wrong and fix it fast.

You don't need to have all the information before you start communicating. In fact, doing so will put you significantly behind. Crises always move quickly and you must be prepared to adapt and change direction as you go. But, most importantly, your organization must show empathy for those affected.

I attended a community liaison session once to discuss a proposal to expand a waste incinerator. The company representative opened the session by telling the audience he was sure they would much rather be down the pub than having to attend such a session. The audience hit the ceiling. How dare he presume to know what they were thinking and why would they want to be anywhere else when there was a chance to hear how proposals would affect their homes and families?

He was heckled relentlessly for the next hour and when the session was over, returned to his car – minus its wheels. The planning application never did get approved and to my mind, it all started from that one inept comment in a community hall at the start of the whole process.

Remember that you chose your organization, so your normal workday ceases to exist until the job of closing out the crisis is done. You owe it to your employer to do whatever it takes to help it through and make sure it never happens again. To my mind, you signed up to this way of thinking when you signed your contract of employment. Duty is an old-fashioned concept these days, but I stand by it.

8. PRESENTATIONS

The purpose of communication is to change behaviour. But it is my experience over the years that giving presentations at work is singularly ineffective in achieving this outcome.

This somewhat controversial observation was epitomized by a presentation I gave to a large and influential audience some years ago. It was the most complete example of its type in my particular work area. The aim was to persuade others across a global business to adopt an award-winning approach my team and I had taken, when they faced the exact same challenge. The argument was compelling. This was a friendly audience with strong relationships and high levels of trust.

At the end, the audience was in full agreement that this approach was a revelation and one that they should take away and use. They concurred with the all-important call to action. It was logical, doable and supported their objectives. Lots of nodding and smiling. The perfect presentation. Job done.

Then nothing. Not one jot of activity in support of this approach by anyone. If ever a presentation was going to change a behaviour, I thought it would be this one. But it wasn't.

I could have seen this as their failing. But I didn't. I saw it as mine. Obviously, I went about it the wrong way. After all, the meaning of communication is the response it elicits, not the intent of the sender. I forgot that the audience of one is more important at work than the audience of many.

So why, in the modern world of work, is presentation-giving such a staple of our daily lives if it is so ineffective?

The efficiency mistake

Typically, presentations are given one to many. One person communicating with many in one hit. There may, of course, be a discussion that ensues. But a discussion is not a presentation. A discussion is a discussion.

The logic must be that giving a presentation is efficient. It saves time. You can speak to several people in one go and not have to speak to them individually. But how can it be efficient if it doesn't work?

Giving presentations is a lazy way of working. When someone asks you to give a presentation what they are really saying is: 'It's your presentation skills that had better be up to the job of making change happen, no matter how good your idea'. And what you are saying to yourself is: 'I will have done my bit and if nothing changes then it's the audience's fault not mine'.

There's also something about presentation giving that feels like procrastination. How many times have you presented only for members of the audience, who may well not actually be decision-makers, to then pick apart your thinking and ask you to go away, do more work and come back later and try again? There is nothing quite like it to sap your energy and enthusiasm. All this, to me, sounds like a technique for failure from the outset.

You can't build rapport easily with a group of people in a presentation setting. The more there are, the harder it becomes. Therefore, your ability to influence them is severely hampered.

That's why when we attend conferences, we attend lots of presentations, then come away and rarely do anything differently. People don't go to conferences to listen to presentations, they go to meet people. That's why more and more people drop out of sessions as the event progresses.

Extending the rapport idea further, as the audience numbers increase, your ability to keep the attention of each one drops off sharply. Different people will be interested in different things. When people attend your presentation with their tablet, phone or laptop out, you like to think they are making notes on your insights. But you know that really many will be catching up on emails instead. Because that's what you do.

You might argue, even at this point, that presentations are more for information sharing. But so what? Even then, shouldn't the ultimate outcome be that someone, somewhere does something differently as a result? Don't organizations thrive on improvement? So, what's the solution to the efficiency mistake?

Identify what it is you want to change. Then seek out the key person who can help make that change happen. Sit down with them face to face and deploy your best influencing skills to get them onside. Then let them help you by exerting their own influence over other stakeholders, if there are any. If you need to win over a few more people, then be properly efficient and speak to them individually. If you need to win over a crowd, then you may want to reconsider what it is you are proposing in the first place. Trying to get a large group of people to agree on anything at work is a fool's errand.

The sophistication mistake

Occasionally, people tell me that this or that presentation we have attended was excellent. And occasionally I agree. But what usually happens is, firstly, we have confused a speech with a presentation or, secondly and more commonly, simply confused style with substance.

On the first point, we probably need some clarification. A speech is not a presentation. Some say a speech uses no visual aids, but a presentation does. But for me it's much more than that. A speech appeals to the emotional. A presentation, the rational. A good speech could make you cry. A good presentation could make you take some notes.

'If you are to go through the pain of giving a presentation, you may as well monster it and come out of the experience as one of those exceptionally rare people with both substance and style.'

So, to stay on track, we are dealing with presentations in this chapter and so I will come to the second point. Some people know how to make their slides sing. Some people are charismatic when out in front of an audience. This combined sophistication enables a multitude of sins in the substance to be hidden or even made to look irrelevant given all the glitz.

When people are standing in front of us talking, we pay little attention to what they are saying. We are consumed with analysing what they look like, how they carry themselves and how they are saying what they are saying. This is normal and well understood human behaviour.

We have all seen the research that says 7 percent of meaning is communicated through spoken word, 38 percent through tone of voice and 55 percent through body language. A presentation is the perfect setting for observing this research in the real world.

Now, clearly some people have the style and the substance to back it up. But in my experience, these people are as rare as hen's teeth.

The reputation mistake

And now to the third and final mistake. Some people also give presentations because they believe it will build their profile and enhance their career. An opportunity to showcase their expertise to a lot of people.

I say that those with talent don't need to shout. Those without, do. You need to decide what kind of employee you are and what you want to be known for before you embark down this 'look at me, look at me' route. Those who can, do. Those who can't, talk about it.

Success lies in preparation and only preparation

The headline of this section is going to need some explaining. Bear with me. I worked for a hugely successful organization a few years ago. They had a unique way of presenting to clients to win work. They used what I will call here a 'talkbook'.

This was a PowerPoint document that broke many of the usual rules in terms of keeping content light. Often the slides were loaded with information, but they were always meticulously and consistently laid out in line with brand guidelines with graphics specialists in support to help.

These talkbooks were effectively a proposal. Setting out the as-is situation, the broader context, a thorough understanding of the issue that needed resolving, proposed solutions, risks and mitigation, resource implications, expertise to help, timeline, fees and a clear articulation of the to-be state. A proper proposal. The preparation that went into these documents was staggering. Then it was used as the basis of a discussion, not a presentation. It was printed, not projected. It was left with the client as a resource for them to read and share with others in their organization. This approach was highly successful. Conversion rates of pitch to sale were tracked daily.

The lesson I took away from this experience was one of preparation and how powerful it is whether the material is actually presented or not. The discipline and rigour of pulling the required information together meant those going to see the client were properly prepared for whatever might come their way.

I work this way if I want to persuade others to adopt my ideas, whether an actual presentation materializes or not. And I have found that my own version of creating a talkbook means that the best presentations are the ones I never actually give.

I prepare as if I am to give one, but then use my talkbook as a discussion framework, something to send to people before a meeting to set the scene and prepare the path, or something with which to follow up a conversation as a prompt for action on any agreed discussion points. Preparation for a presentation is, therefore, more important than any presentation you can give.

Avoiding a dog's breakfast

Now, having said all the above, I am a realist and recognize that sometimes you just need to do what you are asked to do. What happens, if despite your best efforts to steer the approach in another direction, a traditional presentation where you stand up and talk people through some slides is what is asked of you? Well, let us run through some basic rules and make sure we weave in as much of the thinking above as possible to maximize your chances of a positive outcome.

First off, let's reinforce the point about preparation. Do your prep and do it well. Most organizational presentations should set out a thorough assessment of the current situation. Informed by wider business context or external research. You should build in some datapoints to strengthen your position. Your proposal for change needs to come quickly in the slides, setting out with a high degree of specificity what needs to change and why. You may have started with a broader view, but you need to focus fast. You must articulate the end state, what things will be like when your proposed change is implemented and then tie the benefits to the organizational strategy. You should address resources, risks, timeline and budget. Finally, you need to set out the next steps and what you want the audience to do differently straight away after your session. And through all of this you need to dare to appeal to the emotional, as well as the rational.

Now, let's deal with the slides. Our usual weapon of choice for presentations is still PowerPoint. It's a powerful tool in the right hands but in the wrong hands it has all the bells and whistles you could possibly need to make a right dog's breakfast of a visual presentation. I apologize for using such an informal Britishism, but it's the perfect description.

You need to bring your prep to life in a handful of slides that you can present in less than 20 minutes. Even that is probably too long. Remember, people's attention span is short and ability to retain information low. You need to be concise. Slides need to be able to stand up on their own. Remember, people will probably ask for them afterwards or you may want to send them to people beforehand to warm them up, so they need to be clear in what is being said without you having to say it.

Keep slide transitions, animations, images and graphs to a bare minimum. They hinder accessibility. Follow the brand guidelines closely so your fonts, logos and spacings are correct. There's nothing worse than a squashed logo to make you look like an amateur. Have no more than three font sizes on your slides, including the title, and never mix fonts. Be wary of using pale text on dark backgrounds; contrast sensitivity is real for many people and it puts unnecessary strain on the eyes. They won't thank you for that.

Each slide should be numbered to help people navigate and the title of each slide should be the key message you want people to take away. If you just had the slide titles ordered on a piece of paper, it would tell the story you want them to remember. You should see 50 words per slide as a maximum. Talk around your slides to add depth. Pick out highlights. Don't read them.

Finally, think about where you will give this presentation. Go and see the room if you can, so you get a feel for how you will set up so the technology works, how you will use the space and whether people at the back will be able to see what you have prepared or hear what you say.

Now let's move on to you. It's well known that giving a presentation is fraught for many people. Being the centre of attention is not something many of us relish. I've got the jacket to this club.

Once you have completed your excellent prep and created some stunning slides, you will start to feel intellectually bulletproof. Now we just need to make sure you are emotionally bulletproof too.

Rehearsing your presentation is the best way to achieve this. It gives you muscle and neurological memory. Like riding a bike, it will become familiar and less daunting. It helps to quieten your inner critic and remove the distracting asides, as well as the 'ers' and 'ums' that plague us all.

Rehearse your presentation in front of someone who will be able to give you useful feedback. Someone you trust. There is no shame in asking for such help. It shows strength and professionalism. If nothing else, it helps you make sure you are sticking to time.

With each slide have your hook, line and sinker built in. The hook is the unexpected new insight or never-before asked question, the line is the problem afoot and the solution, and the sinker, is the killer blow that sets out why it's important for people to act. Turn up your performance dial: moving from a natural three out of ten to a five or six for presenting.

Remember, you may want to rush through your presentation to get it over and done with. Don't. Breathing is important so don't forget to do it. Take your time, use dramatic pauses and vary your tone of voice, volume and pace to keep people's attention. Imagine you are Richard Burton narrating *Under Milk Wood* by Dylan Thomas or Dame Helen Mirren narrating *Ulysses* by Alfred, Lord Tennyson. Linger longer on the points that matter most.

Scrutinize your audience, meet their eyes in turn. Notice all the details. How are they sitting? Where's the energy in the room? Who's in charge? They will notice and feel that you are connecting with them. You will be building rapport. Don't forget, they want you to succeed. They want you to ace it. Not only for their own benefit, but secretly they know how difficult it is to stand up and talk in front of others. No one likes to see anyone die on stage.

Finally, don't be scared of using appropriate humour. I heard someone give a presentation once when he lost his train of thought early on. He said, 'if it appears that I am fumbling around and ill prepared, then it's probably because I am fumbling around and ill prepared', as he flicked through his notes. The audience roared with laughter and he then had them in the palm of his hand. I can't imagine this working in a boardroom, but people are people and everyone has a sense of humour, somewhere. You'll know when it feels right.

This may all sound like overkill. But let's face it, if you are to go through the pain of giving a presentation, you may as well monster it and come out of the experience as one of those exceptionally rare people with both substance and style.

I was lucky enough to have the opportunity to be coached by a former Hollywood actress to help me overcome my dread of presentations. If presentation giving is a block for you, then the right coach can really help.

9.BEHAVIOUR

DON'T JUDGE PEOPLE'S BAD
BEHAVIOUR TOO HARSHLY

This has been the most difficult chapter to write in this book. I'm someone who tends to look forward, so regurgitating bad experiences is never something I find particularly helpful. But it needed writing, because strained interpersonal relationships remain one of the key areas of work with which people encounter many problems.

So, if this book is to be truly useful for people at work facing similar issues, I need to address it. And again, in the spirit of everything else I have written, to do so by sharing real experiences and ideas that you can use.

Although rare, I have been on the receiving end of some shocking behaviour in my time at work. And I have witnessed behaviour towards others that has defied belief.

But at the same time, despite it never having been my intention, I am sure that some will have believed my behaviour to be lacking on occasion. Not one of us could say with hand on heart that we've never messed up.

This chapter doesn't address the kind of bad behaviour at work that warrants immediate escalation: breaches of your organization's ethical code, compliance, people or safety polices, or even the law. I think we can agree that these issues are far more straightforward to deal with.

Instead, in this chapter we aim to deal with broken relationships, interpersonal tensions, differences and clashes that many of us face quite often at work. It would be odd if we didn't. Some degree of conflict is good, provided it's healthy. But I want to talk here about when it isn't.

Sustaining me through such challenging times has been the desire to never let myself become a victim when I have been on the receiving end. Trying never to judge others when I see what they are doing is damaging. And for my part, always doing what I believe to be right, but being prepared to listen and change my behaviour if I am wrong.

A forgiving heart

I have never come across anyone in all my years at work who wasn't, in their own way, just trying to do their best. That's a bold statement given some of the things I have seen but I have to believe people don't come to work to be monsters, they just make mistakes.

A mentor once asked me to think, no matter how dire someone's behaviour seemed, what their positive intention was towards me. In other words, how were they trying to help me, even if every fibre of my being told me otherwise. And then, most importantly, to act as if it were true.

'The ultimate root of any bad behaviour is always fear. Always. It's just that at work you will experience other emotions from people piled on top of their fear first.'

It's not easy to do. It takes practice, the ability to calm your emotions and step out of your situation. It also demands a forgiving heart. But it is the single most effective way I've found to deal with strained relationships at work.

Acting as if a positive intention were true, as hard as it may be, enables you to come up with new ideas on how to approach tricky situations. It gives you flexibility in your thinking and quietens your emotions, without ignoring them, so you can think more rationally.

Let me show you, by way of three short stories from my career, the power of this way of thinking. Each story a progressively more challenging example. But I want to leave you in no doubt that it works no matter what challenges you may be forced to confront.

Powerplay

I used to write reports for a technical leader. No one much liked him, me included. But let's get one thing straight from the outset. He wasn't just a hard taskmaster. I think we can all deal with those.

This person treated junior colleagues poorly, often undermining their actions or belittling them. He played games with them and set traps for them. He was sarcastic, patronizing and manipulative. He was status driven and liked to show that he was more powerful than others. But we meet all sorts of people in the workplace and I was still wet behind the ears, so I just got on with it and tried my best to avoid him, as any interaction with him would spoil my day.

His focus on me intensified over a few months. Nothing I did seemed to be good enough. He would pick my reports apart bit by bit, using a red pen to vigorously strike through bits he didn't like, shaking his head and tutting like a disappointed headteacher. He made me sit down in front of him while he sat behind his huge desk with his feet upon it. He only looked at me to shake his head.

I listened to everything he said and the next time I did my report I was sure I had it taped. This time there would be nothing he could fault. Finally, he agreed. Only then, at the end of our meeting, to toss it onto the desk and say next time to put the staple at an angle in the top left corner so it was easier for him to turn the pages. He was clearly someone never to be pleased.

Now, I didn't think this way at the time but with magical hindsight and the emotion taken out of it by time and experience I can ask, what was his positive intention towards me?

The answer? He wanted me to be a superb writer of technical reports. Pure and simple. He never said that to me. I am sure he never even thought it, but had I acted as if that were true at the time the whole sorry few months would have made much more sense and been a much more manageable experience. I like to think I am a better report writer even now because of those difficult days, so for that, I thank him.

Plagiarism

My first thought, oddly, was feeling flattered. Someone taking my work, removing my name, then presenting it as their own. Then I became angry, as someone with few of the necessary skills or experiences to succeed, was hailed as a success.

I was older by this point and was practised in seeing positive intentions no matter what. It was a stretch for me to get there, but their positive intention, I decided, was for me to be more forceful in my relationships with others. To step up more and put myself forward. To speak out for myself and not be content with doing good work behind the scenes. I acted as if this is exactly what he was doing. Even though I knew it not to be true. I inserted myself in key conversations across the organization, pushing forward my proposals and ideas more energetically.

People noticed. This was an organization that rewarded people with gumption and who were prepared to take a risk. It was a testosterone-driven environment and in my own way I started to play by their rules.

I had always been successful at this organization with some people but, truth be told, struggled with others. These struggles eased. I was welcomed into places I had never had the chance to influence before.

I knew what I was doing and it worked. I also knew that this person had no such positive intention towards me but acting as if they did made the problem disappear. They had no opportunity to use my work, because I did it before they had the chance.

Gaslighting

At the beginning of this chapter I talked about what you do when the behaviour you witness breaks the rules. A clear violation of your organization's ethical code, a breach of policy or even the law.

The experience I share here was so subtle, so carefully executed that proving it or even raising it felt impossible for me at the time. Hopefully you'll see why. So, I saw no choice other than to deploy my positive intention approach again.

This member of my team would turn up, unannounced, to meetings I had arranged with someone else. Even external meetings. Saying I had invited them, when I hadn't. It turns out they had been stalking my diary which was open to the department, as was the way in this organization.

They would tell me things I had said to them, when I hadn't. They accused me of breaking promises that I had never made. They did work that I had never asked them to do, saying that I had. They didn't do work I had asked them to do, saying that I must have made a mistake. Sometimes they called me a liar. Then they started to tell others. It was a desperately unnerving experience.

I had never heard the term gaslighting at this point. We are much more familiar with it these days as a form of psychological manipulation in which a person deliberately sows seeds of doubt in someone else, making them question their own memory, perception or judgment.

But whatever was happening, I knew it wasn't right. My first thought was perhaps my mental health was suffering. Then I thought perhaps it was theirs. So, what was this person trying to do? And why?

The only positive intention I could come up with was that this was their way of asking me to be clearer and more transparent. A lot clearer and a lot more transparent, so there was no room for misunderstanding on anything. They were seeing secrets when there weren't any, so I needed to remove all chance of them perceiving one.

I went back to basics and treated this team member as if they were a new starter in their first job. They weren't by any means, but I acted as if they were. I micromanaged them to distraction. Every meeting, every call, every report, every decision and every action we discussed. We wrote it all down and used it as a regular check-in. The gaslighting stopped.

In all my years of work, I have found that every single team member I have ever had has wanted ever-more autonomy, to be trusted with yet more responsibility, free to be themselves and shine in their own way. Except this one. And I wasn't prepared for it at all.

I'm not sure everyone reading this will see what I did as a success. It certainly wasn't sustainable, but let me tell you, it felt like a triumph at the time.

Yoda was right

I want to close with one final thought. Forgive me if pop culture sci-fi isn't your thing, but please bear with me. Master Yoda from *Star Wars* said that: 'Fear leads to anger. Anger leads to hate. Hate leads to suffering.'

In my experience the ultimate root of any bad behaviour is always fear. Always. It's just that at work you will experience other emotions from people piled on top of their fear first. This fear will usually be buried so deep that the instigator of the bad behaviour will not even recognize it themselves. Humans avoid confronting their fears at all costs. Fear of failure, fear of rejection, fear of incompetence, fear of perceived weakness.

So, don't judge these people too harshly. It must be awful to have such deep-seated fear eating away at you every day.

10. WRITING

THE WRITTEN WORD MATTERS
MORE THAN YOU THINK

On 9 August 1940, the war cabinet of the British government issued a secret, one-page memorandum to all departments by the prime minister, simply entitled 'Brevity'. In it, the government set out why shorter reports and more concise writing, free from 'officialese' would help save time and allow busy people to concentrate on the priorities.

It lists some examples of woolly phrases 'which are mere padding and can be left out altogether or replaced by a single word'. It then ends with, 'let us not shrink from using the short expressive phrase, even if it is controversial'. Sounds to me like a message many organizations could issue today. It's a much-neglected skill these days, writing. Especially at work.

Whether it's an email, a report, a presentation, a proposal, an article or the multitude of things in between, it's something with which many people struggle. Not because they necessarily think they are bad at it, but because they don't get the results they want. And it's their writing that lets them down.

I'm far from perfect in the way I write. It has taken me quite some time to hone my skills through lots of practice. But I have become a bit of a pedant and am apt to notice bad writing perhaps more easily than others. I am sure in some ways I can even see it coming. It is my experience that disorganized people rarely write in an organized way. But, knowing I'm a pedant, I tend to be quite forgiving. Others, however, can be much less so. People will form immediate opinions about you if your writing is disjointed or if your grammar and spelling are poor. Furthermore, if you can't write in a way that captures people's attention, they may not even bother reading what you write at all.

Some people will say that writing ability at work is all but irrelevant. We're not Victorians anymore, language is evolving too fast, and that email, messaging, texting and social media have changed the way we write so much that it simply doesn't matter. In this chapter I want to show why, in the modern world of work, this couldn't be further from the truth.

More than words

'There is no greater agony than bearing an untold story inside you.'

Maya Angelou

Whether we like it or not, our nature leaks out of us when we communicate. The language we use is the story of our life. It tells others, if they care to pay attention, what we value, what we believe and what we have experienced. For example, I studied mining geology at university so I am likely to use mineralogical phrases in my work-life like 'a rich vein', 'crystallize' or 'gold dust' more than other people might. I can't help it. It's who I am.

In the same way, language is your way of expressing yourself. The language you choose to use opens opportunities in your life or closes them down. Whether you are communicating with others or communicating with yourself. If you tell yourself you can't do something, guess what? You probably can't.

Our success in life relies to a great degree on our ability to communicate. Language, including writing, forms a significant part of that ability. And in writing we have time to pause before our thoughts make it out into the world, a luxury we don't always have when we speak.

The success of any organization is equally dependent on the language it uses and hence, in many instances, the way its people write. Isn't such a precious thing worthy of our special attention?

Work backwards

Albert Einstein said, 'if you can't explain it to a six-year-old, you probably don't understand it yourself'. So, make sure you're crystal clear on the ideas you plan to write about and that you have anticipated the likely questions your audience will have.

Let's think about the most-used, written communication for many of us at work, email. Research indicates that we each receive just over 100 emails every day on average, and send about 40, with worldwide email usage set to grow by about 3 percent each year for some years to come. If we attended to those 100 emails, we are spending around 60 minutes each day or two to three days each month, minimum, dealing with what comes in. People's frustrations with work emails are well documented and your own experiences will probably be no different.

I interviewed a human resources leader in a bank a few years back and asked her what success should look like for her organization's people. The first thing she said was that it shouldn't be an empty inbox. She felt people spent too much time attending to what was fired at them each day. Meaning they had no time to think ahead and were in a constant state of being reactive to the whims of others.

'People are busy ... so find the sweet spot between being concise and capturing your reader's attention with some creativity.'

I am often asked by people how they can become more effective in their email writing and the first thing I say is to think about whether they need to send one at all. When maybe a phone call or popping round to see the intended recipient, if they can, might be more effective.

This is what I mean by working backwards. Thinking about what it is you want to happen as a result of your writing and then using that thinking to decide if, when and how best to write.

I bet most of us think we do this as a matter of course. But I'm not so sure. When we are busy, we just type and send, to get it done. If you ever have your emails ignored, then you can be sure you are not as good at writing as maybe you thought.

This is all about clarity of purpose. It forces you to think about the people reading your email, what their needs are, what will resonate with them and what will encourage them to take action. It also makes you think about when to send an email. Timing, I find, can make all the difference.

People are busy so you need to find the sweet spot between being concise but capturing your reader's attention with some creativity. And it's these basic principles that should guide all your work writing.

Not doing this means, particularly with email, that you will end up looking like someone simply dishing out demands or abdicating responsibility by passing activity and thinking along to someone else. Or what I call a 'chucker'. I once had a colleague whose email subject lines were always 'pls act', rather than maybe something like 'a request for help', a proper chucker if ever I saw one. The tone of their emails followed the subject, usually along the lines of 'I'm busy, you need to do this, it's super urgent, get on with it'. I ignored them all until finally they learned to try some new approaches.

Finally, on email, I have one other useful thing to consider. It's worth a thought as reputations could be at stake. If your email was leaked to a newspaper or online media outlet, would you be able to stand behind what you said? There's no such thing as confidential with email. They are easily forwarded and recoverable, should the need arise. It's a good discipline, to have that short pause and re-read before you send. I worked with someone once who had all their emails on a 60 second delay after hitting send, just to give themselves those few moments after sending to stop it if they changed their mind or forgot something, as so often happens.

Anyway, getting back to the simple tenet of this section. Be clear on what it is you want to achieve, understand the needs of your audience and make sure that what you write is unambiguous, clear, noticed, remembered and acted upon, whatever you are writing. Otherwise, what's the point?

Inspired writing

There's a tension to manage at work between brevity and ingenuity in writing. Brevity, so you get to the point quickly for busy people. Ingenuity, to make your writing have some panache so it stands out. The answer lies, as invariably it does with such tensions, in needing to do both. It's not a case of having to sacrifice one for the other.

Too much brevity leaves no room for context and can, therefore, hamper understanding, positioning or interest, despite what Winston Churchill said at the start of this chapter. Too much ingenuity can lead to over-explaining, stodgy writing, loss of impact, lack of clarity and ambiguity. You need to be creative and find the middle ground. Let me give you six tips which I have found to work consistently well.

A great turn of phrase

A great turn of phrase is a simple way or being both brief, yet impactful. Using creative metaphors or unexpected comparisons allows you to express yourself quickly and imaginatively. Metaphors appeal to the unconscious mind, so can be hugely powerful in bringing about change. Just make sure you don't sink into corporate gobbledygook, as we have all seen how damaging that can be. Writing creatively introduces new vocabulary, perhaps not commonly used in your organization, so what your writing stands out from the crowd and, excitingly, can often reveal new ways of looking at old problems. A great turn of phrase is a difficult thing to learn but practice makes perfect, as well as modelling those with the knack.

Don't ignore emotions

Don't be afraid to appeal to the emotional in addition to the rational. Writing at work tends to steer clear of any emotions, sticking to the facts and the data. But people are emotional creatures and writing in ways that will fire an emotional response can pay dividends. Just make sure it's the response you want.

Use rich language

Use all the senses. Some people lean towards visual language preferences, some auditory and some kinaesthetic. Some people will say a proposal 'looks' good, others that they like the 'sound' of it and others that they are 'comfortable' with the idea. There are a whole host of visual, auditory and kinaesthetic words we use every day. Listen out for these clues and tailor your writing accordingly. For large reading audiences, mix up your writing style in terms of the senses. That way you stand a greater chance of appealing to more readers. The senses offer a rich vein of magnificent words that, used judiciously, will have impact for your readers.

Be easy to read

Readability statistics in Microsoft Word are a little-used asset. The Flesch system for reading ease looks at syllables per word and words per sentence, helping you to write in ways which improve accessibility. You should be aiming for a score of 60 and over to give the best chance of more people being able to understand what it is you have written.

In addition, passive sentences slow reading down, so keep your sentences active. 'We have launched the new performance management process' sounds eminently better than 'the new performance management system has been launched'. You should aim to have fewer than 10 percent of all sentences in any given piece of writing which are passive.

Be yourself

Be conversational in what you write. Write as you would speak, apart from when you are like, basically, kind of, er, not sure what it is you want to say. Also, don't be afraid to break the grammar rules or bring something of yourself to what you write. Someone once told me it was grammatically incorrect to start sentences with the word 'and'. I tend to do the opposite of what I am told, so I start sentences with the word 'and' quite regularly. And it hasn't done me any harm.

Tell a story

From *The Epic of Gilgamesh*, written about 4000 years ago, humankind has been writing down stories to bring people together, to pass on learning and to entertain. If you can tell a story in your writing, no matter how short, it will help keep your reader's attention and make them think more deeply about what you have written.

Boreholes and brothels

Earlier in my career, I was the site manager at a quarry. We needed to make sure that our activities in extracting limestone did not pollute the groundwater. So, in agreement with local environmental regulators, we installed a series of boreholes around the site from which water samples could be taken. Upon completion of the work, I submitted a report to the regulators setting out what we had done, why and the success of the installations on helping to monitor pollution.

This was back in the relatively early days of word processing software as we know it today. The package I was using didn't recognize the word 'boreholes' in its database and so replaced every mention with a word it did. Unfortunately, that word was 'brothels'. And I had missed it.

Some comedian at the regulators decided it would be hilarious to share the report with the local newspaper. Which they duly did. I will leave you to imagine the headline.

The main lesson here, which has stayed with me ever since, is to proofread everything. At least once. And better still, out loud if you can. Everything from a weighty report to the briefest of emails.

Who knew that a section entitled 'boreholes and brothels' would be about proofreading? Hopefully the unexpected wording acts as a good trigger to remind you to proofread your work.

11. MENTORS

IF YOU WANT TO GET ON IN YOUR CAREER, GET A MENTOR

In our time in the modern world of work there will be occasions, inevitably, when despite our best efforts, we feel overlooked. We aren't recognized for our good work and get the impression that we are somehow being exploited, ever putting more in, but not getting any more out.

It's my experience that this happens a lot to people in organizations. At certain stages of my career it has happened to me. I was once part of a team which, through some of the most innovative communications I have ever seen in any workplace, helped accelerate the successful merger between two large organizations. Only then, at the end of it, to be made redundant. Exploited doesn't even come close to how I felt at the time.

At times we are also sure to see others promoted or celebrated in some way for their efforts. Usually it's obvious for all to see why this has happened and it's easy for us to be happy for them. But at other times, not so much. I think we've all been there. But it's a good skill to have the grace to be magnanimous towards these people, no matter what our internal dialogue.

It might now be a cliché, but the *Chicago Tribune* columnist Mary Schmich once wrote: 'don't waste your time on jealousy; sometimes you're ahead, sometimes you're behind. The race is long, and in the end, it's only with yourself'. I've found this to be a helpful maxim in my career.

I'm always curious, though, about the steps people take to become successful, whether it's obvious to me why they were recognized or not. It goes back to the idea of modelling others. What did these people do, specifically, how did they do it, and what can I take away and use for myself?

The one thing that makes the difference

The single most common thread I have found is that successful people at work usually have a mentor. A carefully chosen partner with whom they collaborate, over time, to help them be themselves at work, build their skills, expand their networks, navigate challenges and seek out the right opportunities to speed up their career.

Many of my best career moments have come about because I have been blessed with a mentor right for me at that time. And every time it has been about this mentor daring me to do better. Believing that if I thought about things differently, I could.

Mentoring has grown in popularity over recent years with programmes springing up across many organizations. It makes sense doesn't it? People with lots of experience spending time supporting colleagues with less, to help them grow and become more successful. It's efficiency at its best.

I want to share with you some thoughts that might help you consider this as a good strategy and to then find the right mentor or even get more out of a mentoring relationship you already have.

Making the right choice

Some organizations have formal mentoring programmes and others, much more informal arrangements. Some organizations have no arrangements at all and it's up to each person to initiate the idea and make it happen. I've seen all these approaches deliver results in their own way.

But making it truly work relies entirely upon you finding the right mentor for you. So, don't ask to be given one or let someone else choose one for you. You need to take an active role.

'You want your mentor to ask you questions you are either too afraid to ask yourself or questions that make you think about things in ways you have never done before.'

A mentor is not a line manager and never should be. A mentor is also not a trainer. They may not even be from within your own organization. And I would also suggest that your chosen mentor should not even be from your own work area. This helps avoid the mistake of a mentor being an advice giver. Never underestimate the objectivity someone can bring who is outside your normal sphere of work.

Your biggest pointer in finding the right person is rapport. Someone you get along with, whom you trust and respect. Someone whose skills would be valuable to model. Someone who is well regarded and someone who will ask you the kinds of questions no one else will. Someone who has a genuine interest in you as a person. And, critically, someone who will also benefit from the mentoring relationship. It's a two-way street and, if the mentor isn't also learning and growing as part of the experience, it's doomed to failure.

Which is why I dislike the term 'mentee' for the person who is being mentored. It's become fashionable so you are sure to hear it a great deal elsewhere. But for me, I cringe every time I hear it. It sounds passive. Like a person having something done to them. And that isn't what this is about at all. If there is any doing to be done, then you are doing it yourself. The mentor's role is to help you find your own solutions and open your own doors. Which brings us on nicely to how the mentoring relationship should work.

It's not therapy, but you should treat it as though it were

The kind of person who can successfully mentor others is a rare creature indeed. I see too many people asked to mentor others who are simply ill-equipped to do it well enough.

It's a serious business, mentoring, because we are working with people's lives. We should, therefore, regard it as a therapeutic relationship that requires careful handling. That's not to say that it's therapy, but we must act as if it were.

This means both parties agreeing to engage with one another in a productive, healthy relationship to bring about change. Both parties must be prepared to be open with one another and share their own experiences, good and bad. So, while you may have chosen your ideal mentor, they also need to choose you. It's a humanistic, reciprocal arrangement built on trust and rapport.

And, there must be a built-in mechanism for either side to end the relationship without blame or any sense of failure if it isn't working. You wouldn't choose a bereavement counsellor whom you didn't feel could help you. So, no one should have to suffer a mentor they don't feel is helping them.

While we can be clear that a mentor is not a counsellor, I often hear debate around the concept of coaching. I'm sure many will argue to the contrary, but we can think of mentoring and coaching as the same thing at work.

Some will argue that mentors are there to give more prescriptive advice, whereas coaches are far more non-directive. I want you simply to see your mentor as being a skilled helper, which means them having the flexibility to use whatever techniques work for you. Sometimes directive, sometimes less so and sometimes even content free. But for reasons we will explore next, the latter is usually far more sustainable and effective.

So, you have now decided that having a great mentor is going to be good for speeding up your career. You have identified the best person for you, and they have agreed it will be a fruitful partnership. Now, what are the rules of engagement that you need to consider? I have condensed them for you below.

The five rules

Ask no advice and take no advice

This isn't advice. It's an instruction. We're not in the business of seeking professional advice in a mentoring relationship, so no one should be asking for it and no mentor should be so arrogant to assume that what they would do in any given situation would be the right thing for someone else. The mentor should share stories of their own experiences, but advise you directly? No.

You don't need someone to tell you how to do things. This creates dependency. In time, you should no longer need your mentor. If they are telling you what to do, how can that happen?

You want your mentor to ask you questions you are either too afraid to ask yourself or questions that make you think about things in ways you have never done before. The mentor's role is to help someone with less experience accelerate their learning and development for themselves. Helping you find your own answers is what you are trying to achieve.

This is why having a mentor outside your immediate work area is so powerful. It removes the temptation for them to give advice or for you to seek it.

Take extra care with feedback

Don't accept feedback unless you specifically ask for it. Just think for a moment. How do you feel when someone says to you 'can I give you some feedback?'. Nothing good ever came out of someone making such an offer.

You know what's coming, right? It's not for your benefit, that's for sure. It's for theirs.

People don't ask you if they can give you some feedback to help you. It will be driven by their agenda, not yours. It will be a regurgitation of something this other person has observed, and they feel compelled to tell you to make you feel inadequate. It's a power game that's probably not even a conscious one. All nicely wrapped up in the chocolate box of 'I'm only trying to help you'.

The true art of giving and receiving feedback is being clear on your motive if you do ask for it and making sure that any feedback you do receive is grounded in behaviours that you can control and not in the subjective opinions of others.

Give of yourself

You cannot be successfully mentored if you are not prepared to be open about your own successes and failures. This goes for the mentor too. People can find this difficult in the workplace. It requires courage to talk about weaknesses. For some, it is equally uncomfortable to talk about their strengths for fear of showing off. The more of yourself you put in, the more you will both get out. Your mentor is not meant to be perfect either. Or an expert. They are meant to be good at untapping potential in others. That's all.

What is discussed here stays here

Never share what you discuss with your mentor with anyone and insist that your mentor does the same. If your boss asks how it's going just say great and leave it at that. In time they will see the changes in you. Better to show people your achievements than tell them. This confidentiality forms the backbone of your arrangement with your mentor.

Stay flexible

Will your conversations with your mentor be about personal development or professional development? Or both? Will it be short term or long term? Formal or informal? Regular or as and when? Outcome specific or fluid? These are decisions for you to make. There are no right answers, just your answers.

But it will be normal for things to change as your relationship matures. You are not creating a dependency, so a successful relationship will see you need and want to talk with your mentor less frequently. That's a healthy sign that it's working.

Completing the circle

I'd like to end with the thought that taking control of your mentorship in an active way will result in a better experience for you. This in turn means that you will become far better placed to then mentor others when the time is right. Few of us in corporate life have a genuine opportunity to leave a legacy, but what better one can there be than to have made a positive impact on someone who asked for your help. Like I have said, it's a heavy responsibility to mentor others and it should always be viewed as a privilege to have the opportunity to do so.

12. COMMUNICATION

NOTHING IS REAL UNTIL IT'S COMMUNICATED

In this chapter I want to talk about employee or internal communication. The mechanisms by which employees are kept informed of what is going on, understand what is expected of them and are motivated to improve their performance in line with organizational goals. Thereby becoming advocates who not only stay longer but recommend their employer as a good place to work.

The good news for you is many organizations now have specialists in place to help drive effective internal communication. The bad news, which many forget, is that doing it has always been and remains ultimately the responsibility of those who manage others, no matter what their role. Specialist internal communicators are there to help you do this part of your job well, nothing more.

This might sound odd coming from someone who has devoted a large part of their career to internal communication, but let me show you why this is the case. And let me share with you the skills that I have learnt so you can become a worthy internal communicator in your own right.

Who knew cosmic events would play their part?

My journey with employee communication started in earnest during a solar eclipse. I'd like to say I was somewhere glamorous when the sunlight faded, the birdsong ceased and an eerie blanket of shadow swept across the landscape. But I was in an office car park on the outskirts of London.

As my colleagues and I stood, staring up at the corona through dodgy safety specs we cut out of the local newspaper, I felt a tap on my shoulder. It was my managing director. 'We've got work to do. Let's go,' he said.

He never was one for wasting time at work. He wasn't moved by historic cosmic events either it would seem.

This business was small. But it was sitting on powerful ideas, huge assets and a market that was ripe for expansion. It was run by people with imagination, courage and a deep-seated care for employees.

Over the next few years this business went on an

aggressive and acquisitive expansion programme. Buying businesses to bolt onto its core, expanding into new technologies, new markets, new regions and even new countries. From day one, as a communications professional, I was involved in every idea and every decision, which meant that every decision, in turn, was made with due consideration to the communication requirements.

If this was going to work, we would not only need to take our employees with us, but we would need to rapidly integrate those colleagues from businesses we bought. We wanted them to adopt our values and sign up to our strategy. But we also wanted to make sure that what made these companies great in the first place was never lost and was used to infect the main business with yet more innovation, more entrepreneurship and more daring. We would be stronger together and the way we communicated with our people, old and new, would be central to our success. And you know what? It was. The company I left was unrecognizable from the one I joined. And in an astonishingly good way.

All this at a time when employee, or internal, communication was barely understood as a discipline. I have always felt privileged to have been there at the start of what is now known to be a key enabler of organizational performance and change.

In this chapter I want to explore why internal

communication is so critical to success but also, sadly, show why it so often fails. This isn't designed to address all the nuances of the dark art that is internal communication, but rather a useful analysis of the pitfalls to avoid for those of us involved in any organizational change or simply trying to keep our people motivated and engaged.

After all, effective employee communication is primarily the responsibility of a manager. Internal communicators like me come to work to do ourselves out of a job, enabling others to become exemplary communicators so they communicate well without any need for us. So do your duty and make any internal communicators in your organization border on the unnecessary by being an excellent communicator yourself.

Nothing is real until it's communicated

'The single biggest problem in communication is the illusion that it has taken place.'

George Bernard Shaw

Despite everyone seeming to recognize the importance of good employee communication these days, it's often paid little more than lip service. The mechanisms by which it works are not properly understood, it is frequently not given a central role in the problems it is best placed to solve and many organizations fail to have skilled practitioners in place. And I don't just mean the occasional expert, I mean the skills that need to be built within the management community so that effective internal communication becomes just part of the way business is conducted and not something left to a specialist to sweep up.

How many times in our working lives do we hear that 'communication needs to improve'? So frequently, I would suggest, that it has almost become one of our universal truths in the modern world of work. I bet you've said it yourself and more than once. This is a conundrum that I have wrestled with for a long time.

I have worked in corporate communications, specifically internal communication, for over 25 years in a broad range of sectors, often in global organizations. I have been through mergers, acquisitions, rebrands, major crises, aggressive growth, redundancy programmes, culture transformations, relocations, market collapses and a multitude of change programmes to boot.

Central to navigating these challenges successfully has always been effective employee communication. The simple premise being that if an organization can't take its people with it through change, then the challenges become harder and problems pile up. Employee resistance is a formidable force. And by change I don't just mean the big events that reshape organizations. I also mean the day-to-day changes that steadily erode engagement and performance if not communicated effectively.

Underlying all of this is the realization that there are no such things as communication challenges. Only business challenges. Effective employee communication is central to the solution of a whole host of everyday challenges faced by individuals, teams and whole organizations. After all, nothing becomes real until it is communicated and if it isn't communicated effectively then nothing will change or certainly nothing good.

But we need to go deeper. We need to drill into the facile phrase that communication needs to improve and explore how this throwaway line is used to mask real workplace challenges, many of which are nothing to do with communication at all.

Turning the abstract into the tangible

Let's now take a good look at the semantics. Bear with me on this. In language, the process of nominalization takes a verb, a word of action, and turns it into a noun, a thing. And in the case of 'communication', an abstract thing.

Nominalizations remove action from our lives and often render the owner of the words immobile.

You can see why even the word 'communication' leaves us largely clueless. It's abstract and intangible. What does it mean? There's no strategic rationale to what is being said, messages are unclear, those messages didn't arrive, the audience needs were forgotten? The list goes on. The word communication itself is part of our conundrum.

'If an organization can't take its people with it through change, then the challenges become harder and problems pile up ... employee resistance is a formidable force.'

Incidentally, other nominalizations cause issues in the workplace too. Like innovation, collaboration and empowerment. Who knows what these things truly mean or what you are supposed to do to make them happen? Our heart tells us these things are good, but our head is saying, how do I do that? We are now back in the realms of corporate gobbledygook, and we all know how well that worked out.

So, when we hear that 'communication needs to improve',

or any such similarly imprecise phrase, we are none the wiser as to what specifically isn't working. Or what we need to do to fix it. And while we are here, the word improve doesn't help either. Improve in relation to what, exactly?

We are unclear on those behaviours that need to change and to what standard. Because don't forget, we have agreed earlier in this book that the purpose of communication is to change a behaviour.

So, we need to turn all this abstraction into something real. Something we can work with. Something we can measure. It isn't enough to simply talk about communication. We need more information and more specificity.

A symphony, not a jigsaw

On so many occasions in my career, effective employee communication has been the driver of organizational success. And, conversely, so many times has poor communication been the root cause of failure. It is my experience that organizational changes, of whatever nature, fail for one of three reasons.

The first is structural: The change itself is ill-conceived in the first place, misaligned to organizational strategy, launched at the wrong time, poorly project managed or without the appropriate resources in place to drive it through.

The second is related to the first in the area of resources. But more specifically that communication thinking is not involved early enough to inform and shape the decision itself. Treating communication as simply the post box of pre-agreed decisions is always a mistake. This is what we internal communicators call the 'sh*t into ice cream' moment. When we are given something unpalatable and we are asked to somehow make it attractive. A skilled communicator can make a good fist of such a task but it's rarely a sustainable solution. It's a skill better suited to an emergency to get out of a tricky situation.

The third reason is that the change is not communicated effectively. And at this point we must unpack specifically what that means. It means that either leadership voices are absent, or messages are confused or unclear, or the channels by which messages are delivered are not fit for purpose, or audience needs are neglected, or risks are not identified and mitigated or, finally, there is no measurement to track communication performance, so you know when you have arrived at where you wanted to be.

You need all these components in place. You can't think of this as a jigsaw where you might get the general picture with several pieces missing. You need to think of it more as a symphony. If there are no strings, none of it works. Communication is a process, not a series of disconnected events.

At this point let's pause for a breath. If you're reading this and still thinking that all this communication business sounds like the job of your corporate communications team then I have failed to make the point. Over my entire working career, more communication audits and employee opinion surveys than I can remember have told me that an employee's preferred source of information is always their line manager. And on the rare occasions I see something like an intranet come out as the most preferred source, on further digging we learn it's because the line managers are so bad at communicating their people have given up hoping.

The wrong tool for the job

Our employee communication conundrum is further exacerbated by not having the right skills in place, not only specialist communicators but, more importantly, training managers to be good communicators in their own right. If your organization's health and safety procedures were failing and people were being injured in the workplace, you wouldn't find someone from the tax department to help out. If your sales team was missing targets, you wouldn't ask a company secretary to step in. So why is it that when the way an organization communicates with its people is hindering success, many still rely on managers untrained in communication or resort to using someone from human resources, marketing or public relations to try and sort it out? That's if they chose to invest any resources in it at all.

Internal communication isn't employee relations. It isn't internal marketing and it definitely isn't internal public relations. Before internal communication became a recognized discipline, this may have been forgivable. But today, I don't think so. It's a staggering failure of management.

But as long as organizations keep making this mistake the problems will keep coming. It's another reason why 'communication needs to improve'. Because it simply isn't being done well enough.

It's true that good internal communicators are hard to find. Ask any recruiter. It's because the profile of a stand-out internal communicator is not well understood, other than by specialist recruiters. So, general recruiters or hiring managers often don't know what they're looking for. And hence, they don't find it.

The best internal communicators aren't people who have spent their lives doing communications. They have eclectic careers and are, first and foremost, business people. They understand how organizations work. They are also people who understand the human condition, they have high integrity and have never forgotten what it's like to be a regular employee. They can hold their own with any business leader and are good at seeing how communication interventions can solve organizational problems. They are unflappable, exhibiting grace under pressure. They are people who develop creative strategies in the morning and then roll up their sleeves in the afternoon to deliver them. They see the big picture but always pay attention to the detail. They plan their way out of trouble, focusing on important, non-urgent work. They are advisors, no matter what their level. Finally, they are people who have a good gut feel for things but who also relish immersing themselves in measurement data, because as Albert Einstein once said: 'not everything that counts can be counted, and not everything that can be counted counts'.

Current research indicates that around two-thirds of employees in any given organization are disengaged. They are not actively contributing to the success of their employer. Internal communication was designed to have something to say about that and can always help fix it. Even if you aren't that familiar with internal communication as a discipline you will, I'm sure, understand the imperative of strong employee engagement. We've talked about it before.

Now, all this seems to make good sense. But this isn't a chapter just for internal communicators. Forgive me if so far it has come across that way. But I want to make the point that no matter what your role you can learn from this thinking. The way we speak to people to encourage action matters more than most people think it does. If you manage others, then you can learn from this way of thinking. After all, doesn't the profile of a top internal communicator I set out above sound simply like a strong leader?

The goalposts continually move

The final thing I want to talk about in this chapter is expectations. Employees' expectations go up. It's another one of our universal truths. Give them good stuff, they want more. Make things easy for them, they want it easier yet. Inspire them, they want even more inspiration.

Imagine, so accomplished are you at communicating with employees that if you don't keep improving, your people will see it as failing. But see it as failing they will. It's a conundrum for sure, but ultimately a good one. It just means that you can never sit on your hands and consider your job done.

As an internal communicator I have always seen my first priority to do myself out of a job. By helping others communicate so well my employer doesn't need me any longer. I'm yet to achieve this aim. And not because I or my team don't know what we are doing, before you ask, but because just when we get it right, employee expectations rise and I have to start afresh. I'd use a smiley here if the publisher allowed it.

Never forget, employees don't like to be kept in the dark. They like information, transparency and involvement. Because they want to understand. They want to contribute. They want more context than their employers usually think they need. They can cope with change far better than their employers tend to think they can. Provided they know what's going on. But this all hinges on quality communication which never stands still.

So, internal communication will always need to improve, even if you have avoided all the other pitfalls, simply because you are good at doing it. Sorry.

13. HIRING

In the United Kingdom, we have a long-standing joke that you always wait for an age for a bus and then three come along at once. While the wait can be frustrating, we are much relieved. Three big, red, shiny opportunities to get where we want to go. It's not true, of course, but on the rare occasions when it does happen, we notice and then the myth becomes a reality.

As odd as it may sound, something similar happened to me with hiring people. I'd been waiting for good candidates to come along for months and then, in a matter of weeks, three things happened which forever changed the way I now think about hiring people. Let me tell you that story in this chapter.

Started Monday, left Thursday

I have always found hiring people a tricky business. Such a big decision for all parties and so little time in which to make it and with, comparatively speaking, so little information.

Building teams is central to our success in the modern world of work. As organizations grow, there is only so much you can achieve by doing more with the same. Inevitably we reach a point where we can only do more with more, which means bringing in new people.

Getting it right pays dividends. Getting it wrong is expensive, disruptive, time consuming and leads to avoidable performance issues that can become contagious. For me, it's never really been about competence. It's relatively easy to assess and, if needs be, you can build it. But far more about fit, which you can't.

My wife is from former Yugoslavia. They have an expression there which roughly translates into 'every hole has a patch', meaning everyone has a place that's right for them somewhere, they just have to find it. But finding that place for work is, in my experience, far from easy. And so it is with bringing new people into a team.

A few years before my public transport related revelation, which I will come onto in a moment, I went, as many of us do, to an agency to hire a manager for my growing team. The candidate blew me away. Their track record was exemplary. They interviewed brilliantly and were endorsed by the five other people from the organization they met before joining. They started on a Monday. They resigned on Thursday.

My chief executive berated me. The barrier to entry to this business was high she told me. And once in, we held on to people. How had I messed up, she wanted to know? In all honesty, at the time, I had no answer that sounded good when I said it in my head. So, I said nothing. In hindsight I put it down to fit. They simply didn't fit in with the team they had joined, the organization they had joined or the leader (me) they had joined. It didn't take them long to work it out either.

I'd like to say this was my only bad experience. But it wasn't. I'd hired other people this way and had similar outcomes. Not always, but enough for me to doubt it. Although most lasted longer than the time it takes to work out where the coffee machine was.

The first bus

Let's get back to my hiring experiences and my tenuous links to the bus myth. In a short timeframe, I hired three people through three totally different and unexpected routes. All turned out to be hugely successful hires who have each, in their own way, gone on to do amazing things with their careers.

I have used these three routes since, and only these routes. And you know what? They keep being successful. Could it be that I have unwittingly discovered the secret formula to successful hiring? I doubt it. But you may want to think about these ideas before you pick up the phone to human resources and engage the usual agency to find you someone.

Let's wave down the first bus. It all began with a chance conversation. One of the people who worked in the office facilities team told a colleague of mine that they were looking for something more to get their teeth into at work. They felt undervalued in their current role and they wanted a chance to use their skills to better effect. They wanted a career and not just a job. I met them to find out more.

And what did I find? A multilingual, super-organized, well-qualified, highly creative, completer-finisher who had a powerful way with people and wanted to learn. What were they doing bringing teas and coffees to visitors and tidying up meeting rooms? Not that there is anything wrong with doing that, but they were clearly hungry and capable of so much more.

So, I took the risk. I redeployed them in my team and they flew from day one. They haven't looked back since. In fact, they turned out to be one of the best business writers I have ever worked with.

'Building teams ... getting it right pays dividends, getting it wrong is expensive, disruptive, time consuming and leads to performance issues that can become contagious.'

I always keep my eyes open for such people. It is my assertion that all organizations have similar people hidden away, slowly losing faith, who are uninspired and demotivated. Ready to be simply given the right opportunity with the right team to shine. I have redeployed so many people since, it's now my default. It has always been a success. Without exception.

Have I just been lucky or can it really be that easy? Isn't it true that our first thought is to go externally if we need to hire, when the reality is there are strong candidates already inside if only we know where to look?

Of course, I am not naïve enough to think this is the solution every time. After all, it passes the hiring pain on to someone else. But if more people in an organization think this way then ultimately, we will be topping up at the entry level. Promoting from within. And that's a good thing, while making good use of people's skills for which they will thank you.

And thank you they will. I have been involved in numerous employee opinion surveys over the years and an organization's ability to make good use of its people's skills is nearly always something to improve.

This approach has also worked superbly several times for maternity covers as a secondment. So, taking a risk and hiring or seconding people from within is my first revelation. Repurposing people who are talented but underutilized and undervalued. People for whom the fit is much less of an issue as they already have a good feel for the organization. Seeing the potential in people with ambition, helping them build their skills, giving them space to grow and watching them enjoy the ride.

The second bus

Within days, I was approached by a charity to see whether we would be interested in hosting a graduate intern from a deprived community. The charity sent us several candidates and I would willingly have asked any of them to join us. They were supremely well prepared, polished, eager and optimistic. Optimism is one of the traits I always hire for.

The person we chose was a year out of university with a good degree. They were bright, methodical, thoughtful, tech savvy and hungry for an opportunity to start a career. They had spent the previous year stacking shelves in a supermarket and wanted something to fire their imagination and give them a head start. They had no contacts they could ask for help, didn't have a network in the corporate world and saw themselves as one of so many young people in their acquaintance who just wanted a chance to get in front of people and show what they could do.

This person made an immediate impact. They brought fresh ideas and had an appetite, passion and vision for their career that I had rarely seen before. They then went on to be offered a work extension within another department and then, when their time with us was up, landed a great role at a major organization.

I have been back to this charity several times and had exactly the same experience. And I like to think that people with such a strong desire to succeed, work harder than most to make the fit work.

So, working with agencies or charities that bring people from disadvantaged communities to the fore is the second unexpected way I have found talented people. The diversity of thought alone you will achieve is worth its weight in gold.

As an aside, I really like the whole idea of recruiting

for diversity of thought. I once worked for an organization where no one looked like anyone else, pretty much. But everyone thought exactly the same way as everyone else. The organization went to its tried and tested places to hire people every time and the lack of different thinking was mesmerizing. There was something of Ira Levin's *The Stepford Wives* about it.

The third and final bus

Colleagues in human resources will often advise against it if you are trying to fill a permanent role, but I want you to consider what our HR colleagues call the 'temp to perm' route. Hiring someone on a contract for a set period such as six or twelve months with a shared view that it could become permanent if it works out for all parties.

It's not for everyone, but I have made it work several times with much success. Inevitably, it probably means you will be taking on someone who is a contractor. But that means there is a big pool of people available, as contracting is becoming much more common in our flexible world of work. It is also my experience that many contractors will seek a permanent role if they end up loving their assignment. You just need to be open about the possibility before you start. The other advantage, of course, is contractors will probably be available more quickly too.

This route means that you are effectively extending the interview period, giving you a more sensible and adequate amount of time to assess someone's performance and fit for the long term. And for them to assess how your organization fits with them too. Like I say, not for everyone but please don't dismiss it.

After all, if the first two buses were full, the third would be most welcome, he says, perhaps over-extending what is, let's face it, a dodgy metaphor.

14. ANXIETY

YOUR WORK ANXIETIES COULD
BE YOUR STRONGEST ASSET

Anxiety. It used to be that you couldn't talk about it. And certainly not at work. But, thankfully, times have changed as mental health issues have been coaxed out of the shadows. Looking at the number of celebrities who now talk openly about their own experiences, you might think it has almost become fashionable. But the sad truth is that it's just very common.

The World Health Organization estimates more than 264 million people globally suffer from depression with many of these people also suffering from symptoms of anxiety. Which means about 3 percent of us globally.

If you work in a busy office, well pre-Covid at least, look

up and in eyeshot the likelihood is that one or two people will have mental health issues. And the chances are, you simply won't know. It's rarely visible.

Beginnings

Anxiety is a stalker. It lays in wait and chooses its moment to strike. And so it was with me, making its first few appearances at times of maximum strain in my younger days.

Like a vicious assailant it came out of nowhere and threw me to the floor. It set about trying to pull my thumping heart out of my chest. It shut down my hearing, corrupted my vision, took my voice away, drained my head of blood and turned my internal thermostat to maximum. Initial shock over, it then sat weightily, like an exhausted rhinoceros, on my ribcage intent on squeezing out every last breath I had. It had plummeted me into fear. And it took less than ten seconds to do its worst. If you have experienced this then I am with you. If you haven't, I pray you never do.

My first attack of panic was like a visitation from something totally alien, and I set out, mistakenly, to cut this out of me so it would never happen again. Such was the need to avoid a repeat. It turns out, wanting it simply gone is not how it works.

To be clear, I am lucky. When it happens, it's bad. But for me it happens infrequently and when it does, I always seem to find a way through. Many don't.

What matters for me is knowing my triggers, using my coping mechanisms and recognizing that it actually makes me a better person. And, a recent revelation, it makes me better at what I do at work, but more about that later. Above all though, I have learnt, over time, to accept it as a fundamental part of who I am.

I don't fight it anymore. I just look it in the face and stare it down. One day I hope to see it as an old friend.

Revelations

When we meet new people, we make judgements about them. We can't help it. It's part of our natural protection mechanism. Friend or foe? But we tend to think that everyone else has had it easier than we have. Our own stories are fraught with difficulties. Nobody has been through what we have been through to get here.

And then, of course, as we find out more about people, we realize that life has a way of reaching in and messing things up in different ways and at different times for pretty much everyone. We all have our own story and our problems are real for us, even if others don't see it that way.

You don't have to experience war, starvation, homelessness or disease to know stress. In fact, it's often the case in the world of work, that people who seem to have it all carry some of the heaviest burdens inside. Another successful business leader taking their life is all too common a read in our daily media.

'As we find out more about people, we realize that life has a way of reaching in and messing things up in different ways and at different times for pretty much everyone.'

When I first told people about my anxiety, no one took me seriously. I have a relaxed demeanour or so I am told. Calm on the outside, so how could there be turmoil inside? And what on earth did I have to be anxious about?

But when I went to see a cognitive behavioural therapist for some help, the first thing she did was smile and tell me I was in fine company with many, many people just like me on her books. It was then, and only then, that I started to feel okay about it. It was a revelation for sure, but more a relief.

My anxiety lives inside me. I make it. Prompted by

external factors in many cases, but it is driven by my inner critic and my sometime inability to deal with anger. It turns out my inner critic can be extremely good at making me feel vulnerable and that my easy-going way of looking at the world was burying anger. It was a recipe for damage not least because I was conflating anger and anxiety. If you think about it, they are remarkably similar in what they do to you. Perhaps I shouldn't have been surprised.

This is the way anxiety makes its way into my life. For everyone reading this it will be different. And I say everyone because it is my belief that anxiety is rife: obvious, hidden, buried, ignored, masked or simply waiting for the right moment.

Triggers

When panic hits, I can describe what happens to my body, but it is impossible to describe how I feel. Suffice to say that I hope it can never be weaponized.

Getting to know my triggers has been an important step in managing this condition. There's logic to this disease. There's always a reason and usually, for me, it is something specific. So, if I see a potential situation coming, which as I have better understood the roots of my anxiety I usually can, then I get busy creating a new way of reframing what will happen to remove potential pitfalls.

That used to include avoidance. It was driven by my singular ability to catastrophize about upcoming events. I became expert at catastrophizing and avoiding. This way it meant I would never fall victim to the panic. But it soon became clear this wasn't a sustainable way forward for me or my work.

One of my triggers is about being pushed front and centre by someone else and asked to speak to a group. 'Over to you James to outline the approach' and my heart rate jumps instantly as my first indicator of panic. Quite a trigger when you are a communications professional in a global business.

This is much like stage fright. And we all know how common that is. After all, who really likes making speeches, giving presentations or being the focus of attention? For me though, it's way more than a dislike. It's a bear trap that I need to make sure I don't step on.

So, I manage this by not allowing myself to be pushed. I insert myself into the conversation on my own terms in my own time. I decide when it is time to share my thoughts, not others. If you watch carefully, you will see many people on television such as celebrities, reporters and newsreaders use similar coping techniques.

It's subtle, but I have become pretty good at this now, so many with whom I work would never know. Not least because when it is on my own terms I enjoy speaking to groups and am actually quite good at it.

This has achieved an unexpected benefit. Those dreary meetings full of one-way presentations where nothing ever changes have turned into real conversations where ideas flourish, relationships are strengthened and people feel included.

Endings

My journey has taken me from being someone who occasionally felt utterly hijacked by things out of my control, to someone who started to face it down and got to understand how to manage it, and now to someone who uses it to my advantage. The last point being still a work in progress.

I have used my experiences and learnings to help others present to groups. And it turns out that this is one of the things I am really good at while at work. Over the years, I have helped dozens of people at all levels in all sorts of organizations to go from a terrible or terrified presenter to someone who consistently aces their presentations, and perhaps even enjoys doing them.

I have found some ways to use this condition to help me at work. If you have read this far and anything of what

I have said has resonated, I ask only that you think about how you can use your anxiety to your advantage. I know that might sound ridiculous but it's the best therapy I have found. Apart from maybe one other thing.

Apparently, we each take about 20,000 breaths a day. Anxiety is heightened by a lack of oxygen. In my worst moments by body literally forgets to make itself take in air. It's as if my brain can only cope with so many things and it shuts down breathing to do other stuff.

I spent some time learning basic meditation and breathing exercises, which I have found uniquely effective at keeping me balanced. If I have another recommendation, it would be to invest some time to learn how to breathe properly again and appreciate the stillness it can bring.

This chapter is based on an article I wrote, which was shared to coincide with World Mental Health Day, hoping to further open up the discussion about mental health issues in the workplace. My aim in writing it was that if it helped just one other person then it was a job well done.

I was inundated with messages from people sharing their own experiences and thanking me for sharing mine. But what really stood out was that so many people said how brave I was to talk openly about such a personal issue. Most of the comments on the article were from women. Most of the personal emails I received were from men.

I hadn't realized quite how much stigma is still associated with mental health issues in the workplace, how much more open women tend to be in talking about it and how few men are prepared to share their own experiences. There is clearly more work to do for employers to create psychologically safe environments for their people to talk openly about such a common problem.